Historic Monuments of England and Wales

DAVID and FIONA STURDY

Historic Monuments of England and Wales

J. M. DENT & SONS LTD

Made in Great Britain by
Butler & Tanner Ltd, Frome and London
for J. M. DENT & SONS LTD
Aldine House, Albemarle Street, London

This book is set in 11 on 13 pt Monophoto Ehrhardt

ISBN 0 460 04158 4

British Library Cataloguing in Publication Data

Sturdy, David
    Historic monuments of England and Wales
    Index
    ISBN 0-460-04158-4
    1. Title 2. Sturdy, Fiona
    942   DA 600
    Historic buildings—England

Contents

List of Illustrations 16
List of Maps and Plans 19
Introduction 23

ENGLAND

AVON

Temple Church, Bristol 37
Granville Monument, Charlcombe 37
Stoney Littleton Long Barrow 37

BEDFORDSHIRE

Houghton House, Ampthill 37
Wrest Park, Silsoe 37

BERKSHIRE

Donnington Castle 38
Windsor Castle 39

CAMBRIDGESHIRE

Denny Abbey 39
Duxford Chapel 39
Isleham Priory 39
Longthorpe Tower, Peterborough 39

CHESHIRE

Beeston Castle 39
Chester Castle and Roman Amphitheatre 41
Sandbach Crosses 41

CLEVELAND

Gisborough Priory 44

CORNWALL

Prehistoric and Roman Sites 44
Duputh Well-Chapel, Callington 44
St Catharine's Castle, Fowey 44

Launceston Castle 44
Pendennis and St Mawes Castles 46
Restormel Castle, Lostwithiel 48
Tintagel 48
Scilly Isles 48

CUMBRIA

Brough and Brougham Castles 50
Carlisle Castle 50
Castlerigg Stone Circle 50
Furness Abbey, Barrow 50
Hardknot Roman Fort 52
King Arthur's Round Table and Mayburgh, Eamont Bridge 53
Lanercost Priory 53
Penrith Castle 53
Shap Abbey 53

DERBYSHIRE

Prehistoric Sites 55
Bolsover Castle 55
Hardwick Old Hall 56
Peveril Castle, Castleton 56

DEVON

Blackbury Castle, Southleigh 57
Dartmouth Castle 57
Hound Tor, Manaton 59
Lydford 59
Okehampton Castle 60
Kirkham House, Paignton 61
Plymouth Citadel and Harbour-Tower 61
Totnes Castle 61

DORSET

Abbotsbury Abbey and St Catherine's Chapel 61
Christchurch Castle 63
Jordan Hill Roman Temple, Preston 63
Kingston Russell Stone Circle 63
Knowlton Circle and Church 63
Maiden Castle 63
Sherborne Old Castle 65
Winterborne Abbas Ninestones and Poor Lot Barrows 67

DURHAM

Barnard Castle   67
Castle Deer-House, Bishop Auckland   68
Bowes Castle   68
Egglestone Abbey   69
Finchale Priory   69

ESSEX

Audley End   70
Colchester   70
Hadleigh Castle   72
Mistley Towers   73
Tilbury Fort   73
Waltham Abbey Gatehouse, Entry and Bridge   73

GLOUCESTERSHIRE

Belas Knap Long Barrow, Charlton Abbots   74
Deerhurst   74
Hailes Abbey   77
Kings Wood Abbey Gatehouse   77
Notgrove Long Barrow   77
Hetty Pegler's Tump, Uley   77
Witcombe Roman Villa   77

HAMPSHIRE

Bishops' Waltham Palace   77
Hurst Castle   79
Netley Abbey   80
Portchester Castle   80
Portsmouth Garrison Church   80
Portsmouth Landport and King James Gate   80
Titchfield Abbey   82

ISLE OF WIGHT

Appuldurcombe House   82
Carisbrooke Castle   82
St Catherine's Chapel, Chale   83
Osborne House   83
Yarmouth Castle   83

HERTFORDSHIRE

Berkhamsted Castle   84
St Albans (Verulamium) Roman Walls   84

HUMBERSIDE

Burton Agnes Manor House	85
Howden Church	85
Skipsea Castle	85
Thornton Abbey	85

KENT

Horne's Place Chapel, Appledore	85
Kit's Coty House and Little Kit's Coty House, Aylesford	85
St Augustine's Abbey and St Pancras Church, Canterbury	86
Deal Castle and Walmer Castle	87
Dover Castle	87
Dymchurch Martello Tower	90
Ebbsfleet Cross	90
Eynsford Castle	90
Lullingstone Roman Villa	90
Maison Dieu, Ospringe	91
Old Soar Manor, Plaxtol	91
Reculver Roman Fort and Anglo-Saxon Church	91
Richborough Roman Fort and Town	93
Rochester Castle	93
Temple Manor, Strood	95
Upnor Castle	95
West Malling Tower	96

LANCASHIRE

Salley	96
Warton	96
Whalley	96

LEICESTERSHIRE

Ashby de la Zouche Castle	96
Kirby Muxloe Castle	97
Jewry Wall, Leicester	97
Lyddington Bedehouse	97

LINCOLNSHIRE

Bolingbroke Castle	98
Bishop's Palace, Lincoln	98

LONDON

Apsley House	98
Chelsea Hospital	98
Chiswick House	99
Eltham Palace	99
Greenwich Palace and Park	99
Ham House	99
Hampton Court and Parks	100
Hyde Park and Kensington Palace	100
Kew Palace and Gardens	100
Lancaster House	101
Marlborough House	101
Osterley House	101
Regent's Park	101
Richmond Park	101
St James's Park and Buckingham Palace	101
Tower of London	103
Westminster Palace	104
Whitehall	104

NORFOLK

Baconsthorpe Castle	107
Berney Arms Windmill, Reedham	107
Binham Priory and Cross	108
Blakeney Guildhall	108
Caister-by-Yarmouth	108
Castle Acre Priory and Castle Gate	108
Castle Rising	109
Creake Abbey	109
Greyfriars, Great Yarmouth	109
Small Houses, Great Yarmouth	109
Grime's Graves, Weeting	110
North Elmham Saxon Cathedral	110
Cow Tower, Norwich	111
Thetford Priory	111
Thetford Warren Lodge	111
Weeting Castle	111

NORTHAMPTONSHIRE

Eleanor Cross, Geddington	111
Chichele College, Higham Ferrers	111

Kirby Hall	111
Rushton Triangular Lodge	111

NORTHUMBERLAND

Berwick on Tweed	113
Brinkburn Priory	113
Dunstanburgh Castle	113
Holy Island of Lindisfarne	115
Norham Castle	116
Warkworth Castle	116

HADRIAN'S WALL	118

NOTTINGHAMSHIRE

Mattersey Priory	124
Rufford Abbey	124

OXFORDSHIRE

Abingdon County Hall	124
Deddington Castle	124
Minster Lovell House	125
North Leigh Roman Villa	125
Rycote Chapel	125
Uffington Castle and White Horse	127
Waylands Smithy, Ashbury	127

SHROPSHIRE

Acton Burnell Castle	128
Langley Chapel, Acton Burnell	128
Boscobel House and White Ladies Priory	128
Buildwas Abbey	128
Haughmond Abbey	128
Lilleshall Abbey	128
Mitchell's Fold Stone Circle, Chirbury	128
Moreton Corbet Castle	128
Old Oswestry	128
Wenlock Priory	129
Wroxeter (Uriconium) Roman Baths	129

SOMERSET

Cleeve Abbey	130
Dunster	130

Farleigh Hungerford Castle   130
Glastonbury Abbey   132
Muchelney Abbey   133
Nunney Castle   136
Stanton Drew Stone Circles   136

STAFFORDSHIRE

Croxden Abbey   136
Wall Roman Baths   137

SUFFOLK

Burgh Castle Roman Fort   137
Bury St Edmund's Abbey   139
Framlingham Castle   139
Herringfleet Priory   139
Leiston Abbey   139
Lindsey Chapel   141
Orford Castle   141
Saxtead Green Windmill   141

SURREY

Farnham Castle   141
Waverley Abbey   141

SUSSEX
                                               141
Bayham Abbey   142
Hurstmonceaux Castle   142
Pevensey Castle

TYNE AND WEAR

Hylton Castle   143
Jarrow Monastery   143
Tynemouth Priory   143

WARWICKSHIRE

Kenilworth Castle   145

WILTSHIRE

Prehistoric Sites   145
The Avebury Region   148
The Stonehenge Region   152

Abbey Barn, Bradford on Avon   155
Bratton Camp and White Horse   156
Ludgershall Castle and Cross   156
Netheravon Dovecot   156
Old Sarum   157
Old Wardour Castle   157

WORCESTER AND HEREFORD

Arthur's Stone, Dorstone   160
Goodrich Castle   160
Mortimer's Cross Watermill, Lucton   161
Rotherwas Chapel, Hereford   161

NORTH YORKSHIRE

Aldborough Roman Town   161
Byland Abbey   161
Easby Abbey   164
Fountains Abbey   164
Helmsley Castle   166
Kirkham Priory   166
Middleham Castle   166
Mount Grace Priory   168
Richmond Castle   169
Rievaulx Abbey   169
Scarborough Castle   169
Spofforth Castle   172
Stanwick Oppidum   172
Steeton Hall   172
Wheeldale Moor Roman Road   172
Whitby Abbey   172
Clifford's Tower, York Castle   173

SOUTH YORKSHIRE

Conisbrough Castle   173
Monk Bretton Priory   173
Roche Abbey   173

WALES

CLWYD

Basingwerk Abbey	179
Chirk Castle	179
Denbigh Castle, Town Walls and Churches	179
Derwen	179
Ewloe Castle	179
Flint Castle	179
St Winifred's, Holywell	179
Rhuddlan Castle	180
Valle Crucis	180
Whitford Cross	180

DYFED

Carew Cross	181
Carreg Cennen Castle	181
Cilgerran Castle	181
Kidwelly Castle	181
Bishop's Palace, Lamphey	182
Llanstephan Castle	183
Llawhaden Castle	183
Pentre Ifan Burial Chamber	183
Bishop's Palace, St David's	183
St Non's Chapel, St David's	183
St Dogmael's Abbey	183
Strata Florida	185
Talley Abbey	185

MID GLAMORGAN

Newcastle Bridgend	185
Caerphilly Castle	185
Coity Castle	186
Ewenny Priory	186
Ogmore Castle	187

SOUTH GLAMORGAN

Castell Coch	187
Old Beaupre Castle	189
St Lythans Burial Chamber	189
Tinkinswood Burial Chamber	189

WEST GLAMORGAN

Loughor Castle	189
Margam Stones Museum	189
Neath Abbey	189
Parc Le Breos Burial Chamber	192
Swansea Castle	192
Weobley Castle	192

GWENT

Caerleon	192
Caerwent	194
Chepstow Castle	194
The Port Wall, Chepstow	194
Llanthony Priory	194
Llantilio Crossenny	196
Monmouth Castle	196
Newport Castle	197
Raglan Castle	197
Runston Chapel	197
The Three Castles—Grosmont, Skenfrith, White Castle	197
Tintern Abbey	199

GWYNEDD

Early Prehistoric Sites, Anglesey	199
Beaumaris Castle, Anglesey	201
Caernarfon Castle	202
Caernarfon (Segontium) Roman Fort	204
Capel Garmon, Llanrwst	204
Castell y Bere	204
Conwy Castle	205
Cricieth Castle	208
Cymmer Abbey	208
Dinorwic Slate Quarry	208
Dolbadarn Castle	208
Dolwyddelan Castle	209
Dyffryn Long Barrow	209
Fedw-Deg	209
Gwydir Uchaf Chapel	209
Harlech Castle	209
Llangar	210

Llangybi   210
Penarth Fawr   210

POWYS

Brecon Gaer   210
Bronllys Castle   210
Bryntail Lead Mine   210
Dolforwyn Castle   210
Montgomery Castle   210
Tretower Castle and Court   211

Index   213

Illustrations

Wrest Park, Bedfordshire: garden pavilion	37
Donnington Castle, Berkshire: engraving	38
Isleham Priory, Cambridgeshire (*National Monuments Record*)	40
Beeston Castle, Cheshire	41
Agricola Tower, Chester Castle, Cheshire (*National Monuments Record*)	42
Sandbach Crosses, Cheshire (*National Monuments Record*)	43
Duputh well-chapel, Cornwall (*B. T. Batsford*)	45
Launceston, Cornwall (*National Monuments Record*)	46
St Mawes Castle, Cornwall (*B. T. Batsford*)	47
Restormel Castle, Cornwall (*National Monuments Record*)	49
Tintagel Castle, Cornwall (*National Monuments Record*)	49
Brough Castle and Roman fort, Cumbria (*National Monuments Record*)	51
Carlisle Castle, Cumbria (*National Monuments Record*)	51
Castlerigg Stone Circle, Cumbria	52
Lanercost Priory, Cumbria (*B. T. Batsford*)	54
Hardwick Old Hall, Derbyshire (*National Monuments Record*)	57
Peveril Castle, Derbyshire (*National Monuments Record*)	58
Plymouth Citadel, Devon (*National Monuments Record*)	62
Christchurch Castle, Dorset	64
Knowlton Church, Dorset (*National Monuments Record*)	64
Maiden Castle, Dorset: engraving	65
Maiden Castle, Dorset	66
Barnard Castle, Co. Durham	68
Finchale Priory, Co. Durham	69
Audley End, Essex: plan of grounds	71
Audley End, Essex: doll's house	72
Tilbury Fort, Essex	74
Building inscriptions: Roman, Anglo-Saxon (*Ashmolean Museum*), Elizabethan	76
Netley Abbey, Hampshire	79
Portsmouth Garrison Church, Hampshire	81
Carisbrooke Castle, Isle of Wight	83
St Augustine's Abbey, Canterbury, Kent	86
Dover Castle, Kent	88

Reculver Church, Kent: engraving 92
Reculver Church, Kent 92
Upnor Castle, Kent 95
Ashby de la Zouche Castle, Leicestershire 96
Chiswick House, London 99
Hampton Court, London 100
St James's Park, London 103
Jewel Tower, Westminster Palace, London 105
Jewel Tower during excavations in 1962 105
Berney Arms Windmill, Norfolk 107
Castle Acre Priory, Norfolk 108
Grime's Graves, Norfolk 110
Rushton Triangular Lodge, Northamptonshire 112
Berwick on Tweed, Northumberland 112
Castle and Royal Border Bridge, Berwick on Tweed 113
Brinkburn Priory, Northumberland: engraving 114
Dunstanburgh Castle, Northumberland 114
Norham Castle, Northumberland 117
Norham Castle: south curtain wall 117
Chesters Roman Fort, Hadrian's Wall, Northumberland 121
Corbridge Roman Bridge, Hadrian's Wall 123
Housesteads Roman Fort, Hadrian's Wall 123
Minster Lovell House, Oxfordshire: engraving 125
Minster Lovell House, Oxfordshire 126
Uffington Castle and White Horse, Oxfordshire
    (*Ashmolean Museum*) 127
Wenlock Priory, Shropshire 128
Cleeve Abbey, Somerset 131
Glastonbury Tribunal, Somerset 133
Abbot's Parlour, Muchelney Abbey, Somerset 134
Stanton Drew, Somerset 137
Bury St Edmund's Abbey, Suffolk: engraving 138
Bury St Edmund's Abbey, Suffolk 138
Orford Castle, Suffolk 140
Pevensey Castle and Roman fort, Sussex 142
Tynemouth Priory, Tyne and Wear: engraving 144
Avebury, Wiltshire, in 1724 147
Avebury, Wiltshire 149
Avebury, Silbury Hill and West Kennet
    Long Barrow (*Ashmolean Museum*) 150
Stonehenge, Wiltshire: engraving 155

Abbey Barn, Bradford on Avon, Wiltshire 156
Old Sarum, Wiltshire (*Ashmolean Museum*) 158
Old Wardour Castle, Wiltshire 159
Goodrich Castle, Worcester and Hereford 160
Byland Abbey, North Yorkshire 163
Fountains Abbey, North Yorkshire 165
Kirkham Priory, North Yorkshire 167
Kirkham Priory, North Yorkshire: detail 167
Mount Grace Priory, North Yorkshire 168
Richmond Castle, North Yorkshire, in its setting at
   the edge of the moors 170
Richmond Castle, North Yorkshire 170
Scarborough Castle, North Yorkshire 171
Wheeldale Moor Roman Road, North Yorkshire 172
Roche Abbey, South Yorkshire 174
Flint Castle, Clwyd 180
Lamphey Palace, Dyfed 182
St David's Palace, Dyfed 184
Talley Abbey, Dyfed 184
Ogmore Castle, Mid Glamorgan 186
Old Beaupre Castle, South Glamorgan, in 1951 and 1964 188
Margam Abbey Museum, West Glamorgan 190
Parc Le Breos burial chamber, West Glamorgan 191
Weobley Castle, West Glamorgan 191
Caerwent Roman town, Gwent 193
Chepstow Castle, Gwent 195
Llanthony Priory, Gwent 195
Raglan Castle, Gwent 196
Skenfrith Castle, Gwent 198
Bryn Celli Ddu burial mound, Anglesey 200
Bodowyr burial chamber, Anglesey 201
Caernarfon Castle, Gwynedd 203
Caernarfon Castle, Gwynedd: Queen's, Chamberlain
   and Black Towers 205
Castell y Bere, Gwynedd 206
Dolbadarn Castle, Gwynedd 209
Bryntail lead mine, Powys 211

Maps and Plans

Historic monuments in the care of the Department of the
   Environment   22
Norman churches: (*a*) Lilleshall, (*b*) Castle Acre, (*c*) Roche,
   (*d*) Rievaulx, (*e*) Bury St Edmund's   24
Cloister-buildings: (*a*) Whitby, (*b*) Netley, (*c*) Easby, (*d*) Wenlock   27
Major fortresses: (*a*) Iron Age fort: Maiden Castle, (*b*) Roman fort:
   Caerleon, (*c*) castle and town: Conwy, (*d*) bastioned fortress:
   Berwick   28
Castles: (*a*) Totnes, (*b*) Middleham, (*c*) Kirby Muxloe, (*d*) Deal   29
Small castles and strong residences: (*a*) Eynsford, (*b*) Longthorpe,
   (*c*) Tretower Court, (*d*) Nunney, (*e*) Baconsthorpe   30
England: historic monuments of London and the South   32
England: historic monuments of the Midlands and the North   34
Map of the south-west of England   60
Map of the south of England   78
Dover: the castle, town and harbour from a plan of 1737   89
Coastal defences of east Kent   94
St James's Park, London   102
Map of the south-east of England   106
Map of the far north of England   115
The Stonehenge area   153
Map of the north of England   162
Wales: historic monuments   176
Map of Wales   178
North Wales: the Roman conquest and the English conquest   207

Acknowledgments

The photographs are Crown Copyright (reproduced with the permission of
the Controller of Her Majesty's Stationery Office) unless they are acknow-
ledged separately in the list of illustrations.

To

Torald, William and Conan

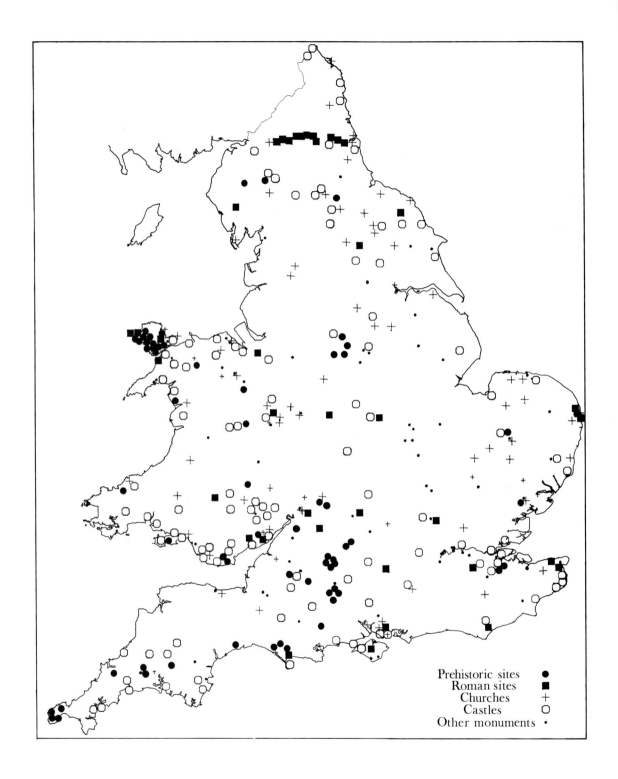

Prehistoric sites	●
Roman sites	■
Churches	+
Castles	○
Other monuments	·

Introduction

This book describes the historic sites and monuments in the care of the Department of the Environment, 'remnants of history which have casually escaped the shipwreck of time'. It is not a very clearly defined group of monuments, except that almost all of them have lost their proper use. There are many ruined abbeys, but no working churches. There are several ruined mansions, but very few houses that are still roofed. Houses in the National Trust's care are not mentioned here, although some of their early sites are. Local authorities and private owners too very often appreciate and share their monuments with the public, and there are more than enough of these to fill another book.

People have always gone around looking at places and the owners and occupiers have usually done their best to help them. Many people in the past have noted what they saw or were told. In the fifteenth century William Worcestre toured East Anglia and southern England, pacing out all the abbeys, jotting down the local stories. Just after the dissolution of the monasteries in Henry VIII's time John Leland went round the whole country, with a Commission from the King, commenting, describing, endlessly concerned with the change that the country was passing through, and noting, with an archivist's eye, the masses of early books and papers that were thrown on the market.

At the end of the sixteenth century, under Elizabeth and her chief minister Lord Burghley, the discovery of England was part of the stimulus and ferment of the time. In the 1560s Laurence Nowell, soon to be Dean of Lichfield, mapped the country in manuscript. In the 1570s Christopher Saxton, a Yorkshire surveyor, followed him, putting in all the villages and getting it all into print with his series of county maps of 1574–9. William Camden published his *Britannia* in 1586, an attempt to say, from his travels, how we came to be what we were. They were an extraordinary generation who could see the value of the past and take a longer view far better than we can. Nowell's maps were at once the most up-to-date official survey, with a numbered grid very close to the National Grid, and at the same time a critical historical analysis, with many names in Anglo-Saxon characters. Across them Lord Burghley wrote in the names of the chief local landowners. How close these studies were to the heart of government is very clear from Burghley's copy of Saxton in which he wrote, the year before the Spanish Armada, county by county along the south coast every figure he could find for cannon, powder, militia and local commanders.

1 Historic monuments in the care of the Department of the Environment

23

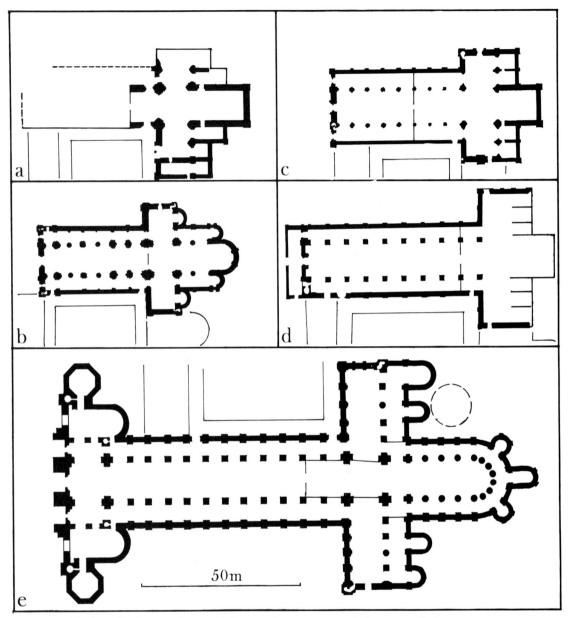

50m

Also at this time the first local descriptions and surveys were being compiled, and William Lambard's *Perambulation of Kent* was the first to be published, in 1576. New editions of Camden's *Britannia* came out in 1600 and 1607—still in Latin—but in English in 1610.

In 1617 Fynes Moryson followed with his *Itinerary*, an early piece of sociology matched in 1630 by John Weever's *Monumental Inscriptions*, which we would

Norman churches:
(a) Lilleshall (page
28), with stepped
chapels characteristic
of Augustinian canons'
churches—about AD
1148, nave later; (b)
Castle Acre (page
108), planned for
Cluniac monks about
1090 with complex
apsidal plan from
Cluny; (c) Roche
(page 173), laid out in
1147 for Cistercians
beside the rocky cliff
that gave the abbey its
name; (d) Rievaulx
(page 169), a great
Cistercian mission
centre started in 1131,
with the short chancel
and severe plan of the
mother churches in
Burgundy; (e) Bury St
Edmund's (page 139),
the great Benedictine
abbey-church with its
earlier Anglo-Saxon
round church

look on as family or area studies. The seventeenth century saw many books on what you can see. In 1675 the first road atlas was published by John Ogilby, with a miniature edition in 1699. In 1695–6 Celia Fiennes was an early and acute commentator on sights and journeys.

A well-illustrated account of landscapes and sites is William Stukeley's *Itinerarium curiosum* of 1724, and later in the eighteenth century William Gilpin searched for the picturesque, and Arthur Young for farming knowledge. Johnson and Boswell, Pennant and many other well-known writers over the years have contributed to our knowledge of our own country.

The Department of the Environment's collection of state-owned or state-run monuments was begun in 1882, earlier than the National Trust, an independent body which goes back to 1895. National Parks have been created since an Act of Parliament of 1949, and are now co-ordinated by a government agency, the Countryside Commission. Ancient Monuments in private hands have been scheduled since 1913; historic buildings have been listed since 1947 and Conservation Areas have been designated since 1969. There ought to be far closer liaison between the various authorities. No official map shows both Listed Buildings and Conservation Areas, let alone Guardianship and Scheduled Ancient Monuments as well.

The Ancient Monuments Protection Act of 1882 followed a nine-year campaign in Parliament, and was constantly denounced as interference in the rights of private property. This early and hesitant essay in nationalization was followed by the Ancient Monuments Consolidation and Amendment Act of 1913 when medieval monuments and an element of compulsion were introduced. This led to the appointment of full-time staff in the Office of Works who have developed into the Ancient Monuments and Historic Buildings Directorate of the Department of the Environment.

These historic monuments are distributed very unevenly both in time and on the ground, as can be seen from the maps on pages 32–3, 34, and 176. There are major treasures of European significance, including the prehistoric sites of Wiltshire, Hadrian's Wall, the 'Saxon Shore Forts', the North Wales castles and the London palaces. There is also a strange selection of foundlings, abandoned at each Chief Inspector's door. Medieval and later monuments form about 70 per cent of the total number, and heavily outnumber Roman and prehistoric sites, some of which are very small and fragmentary. It would be good to see whole early environments interpreted for the public. Prehistoric sites in guardianship are massively concentrated in Wiltshire and the surrounding counties, and in Anglesey (see pages 145 and 199). Roman sites are pre-eminently in the far north and round the south-east coast. In Wales and in the south the emphasis is strongly on castles; Yorkshire has the most superb abbeys.

The settings of the monuments must be a matter of constant concern. Stonehenge is a nightmare of barbed wire, of overkill by people. Army camps, traffic and modern plantations are far too obtrusive. Could the main roads be entirely diverted, and the National Trust estate put down to grassland? At Maiden Castle, the 'finest prehistoric fortress in the country', the newest suburbs of Dorchester obtrude disastrously, and show what little realization the local planners have of their assets. At Knowlton, also in Dorset, there should be marker stones rather than a wire fence round the henge-monument, sheep rather than a whining motor-mower and a hobgoblin by the church instead of a DoE van parked slap in the middle.

Roman forts are very difficult to present and tidy rows of foundations with various alterations can be strangely puzzling when partially displayed or in an incongruous modern setting. To the Romans they must have seemed no more than well-planned military bases, and in Saxon times it must have been great fun pulling down walls at random and looting about for good stone. Their relevance in our day must be more than this unsophisticated playing and wondering. They can tell us of change and of continuity. The coastal forts from Hampshire to Norfolk have, almost all of them, Roman walls, Saxon churches and Norman castles. From the fourth to the twelfth centuries AD they were each of them the centre of a district and are key sites for the whole development of society in that time. Portchester has lately produced, from large-scale excavation, the most fascinating stages of this process of change. Each of the forts needs to be put in a wider setting of the estate farmed from it, the area governed from it and the district that went to church there. All the archaeological sites around, from Roman to medieval, need to be plotted to make a wider sociological study.

Of the Saxon period, the most elusive and difficult to find as standing remains, we need more. There should be a special effort to display more of this period. The partial foundations of St Augustine's Abbey at Canterbury, the chapel at Deerhurst, the church in Dover Castle and the remains at North Elmham, Reculver and Jarrow, the results of excavation at Lindisfarne, Richborough and Whitby, and the crosses at Sandbach and St Cleer are a very scant dozen monuments to 600 years of history. There are personal associations for many of these places; Augustine, Bede, Aidan and Cuthbert need to be figured for us with skill and imagination. We can learn from them too, for they made improvements in a world that was breaking up.

The medieval period gives us more than earthworks and foundations: we have buildings and people to deal with. We have tried, however summarily, to suggest that every visitor to a monument can teach us something new by working out the family connections and social position of the castle, priory, manor or farm. Is there, for instance, a family solidarity among the abbeys

3 Cloister-buildings: (a) Whitby (page 172), Anglo-Saxon with Norman church in outline; (b) Netley (page 80), a typical Cistercian plan with frater at right angles to cloister; (c) Easby (page 164), where the dorter had to be moved from the usual place by the chapter-house to get the water-supply to the latrines; (d) Wenlock (page 129), the most usual plan in the Cluniacs' regular layout:
A—Abbot's lodging,
B—Brewhouse,
C—Chapter-house,
D—Dorter (dormitory),
E—Entry,
F—Frater (dining-hall),
G—Guest-hall,
H—Handwashing fountain (*lavatorium*),
I—Infirmary,
K—Kitchen,
L—Latrine (*reredorter*), as in AD 800 (a), and in 1250 (b, c and d)

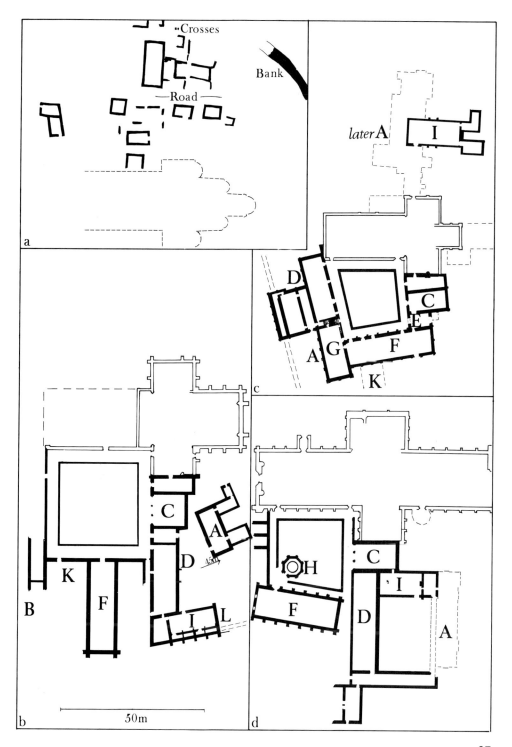

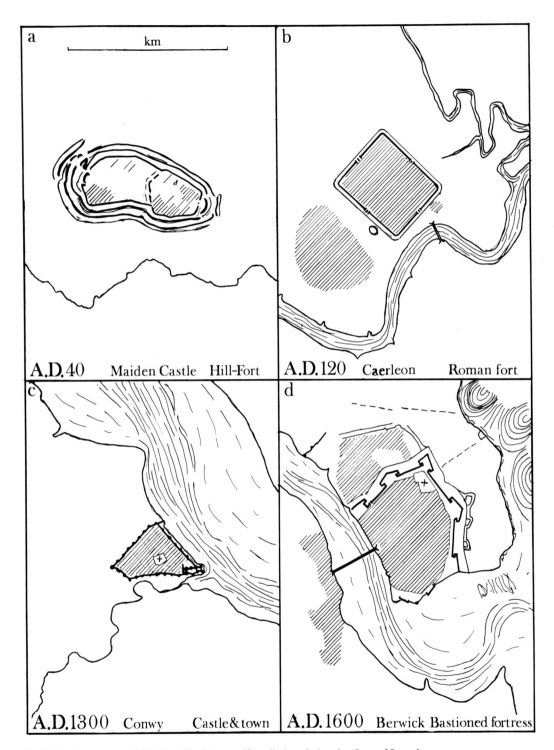

a   km

A.D.40   Maiden Castle   Hill-Fort

b

A.D.120   Caerleon   Roman fort

c

A.D.1300   Conwy   Castle & town

d

A.D.1600   Berwick Bastioned fortress

4   Major fortresses: (*a*) Maiden Castle (page 63), tribal capital and refuge of Iron Age date; (*b*) Caerleon (page 192), base of the Twentieth Legion of Augustus, up to 10,000 strong, focus of the Roman garrisons of South Wales; (*c*) Conwy (page 205), base for Edward I's hold on North Wales, with a normal garrison of 30 and a town of English colonists; (*d*) Berwick on Tweed (page 113), Queen Elizabeth's frontier fortress against the Scots

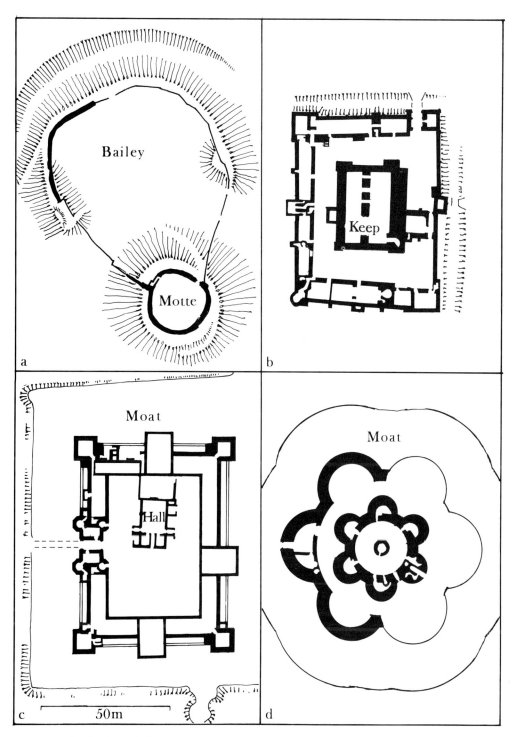

5 Castles: (*a*) Totnes (page 61), an early earthwork castle of about AD 1080 and later stone walls; (*b*) Middleham (page 166), a stone keep of about 1170 with low surrounding ranges of chambers, kitchens, etc., built in the thirteenth to fifteenth centuries; (*c*) Kirby Muxloe (page 97), a 'show' castle lapped round an earlier manor-house in 1480–4, but never finished; (*d*) Deal (page 87), an artillery fort of 1539–40

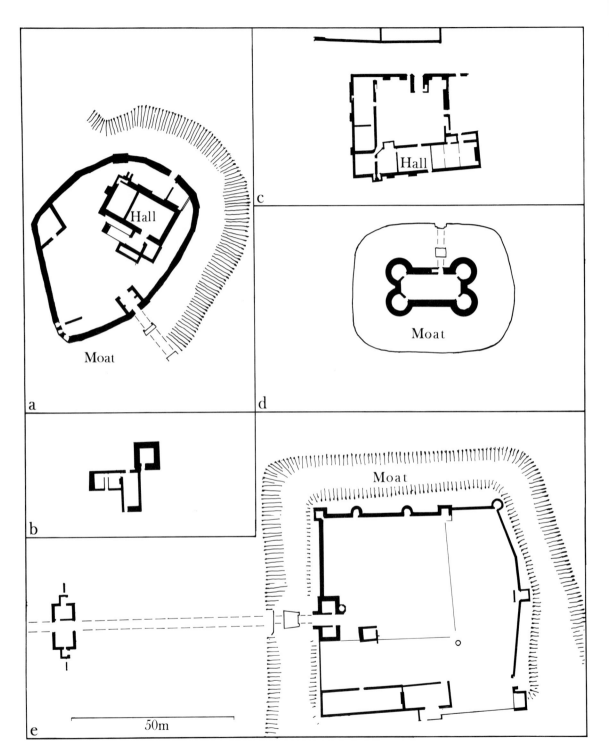

Small castles and
strong residences: (*a*)
Eynsford (page 90), a
baron's stronghold of
0 1100, with central
tower rebuilt as a
strong hall-house in
140; (*b*) Longthorpe
page 39), an abbey
steward's hall, with
tower-like chamber-
block added in about
300; (*c*) Tretower
Court (page 211), a
ew house of the
fourteenth and
fteenth centuries
built some distance
from the older castle;
/) Nunney (page
36), an unusual small
astle or tower-house
f French pattern
built with permission
iven in 1373; (*e*)
aconsthorpe (page
07), a manor-house
rtified, without
ermission, in the late
fteenth century with
later outer gatehouse

founded by William the Conqueror's innermost circle of barons? We have William de Warenne at Castle Acre (page 108) and Roger of Montgomery at Wenlock (page 129), both drawing inspiration from Cluny in Burgundy. What can we find in common among their castles? We can still see William FitzOsbern's palace-tower at Chepstow (page 194) and Count Alan of Brittany's hall range at Richmond (page 169). How do these compare with the Conqueror's own great Tower at London (page 103)? Later we can ask what skills Henry II's advisers brought back from the Holy Land to use on Dover (page 87) or Scarborough (page 169). There are a hundred social and economic, political and military, religious and personal problems that have never been worked out.

We have dealt very briefly with the monuments in London which are mostly palaces of the sixteenth to eighteenth centuries, still roofed and generally distinct from the run of sites in guardianship.

For dates we have followed the best authorities, but many medieval dates depend on casual references or uncertain identifications. New information can allow us to push a building or an alteration twenty or fifty years either way. Prehistoric dates are now a matter of extreme uncertainty. Scientific techniques of radiocarbon dating have given us strings of figures that mean something, but they are still in the middle of being 'recalibrated' as new factors emerge and have to be allowed for. We have put only very broad dates down, since they will be obsolete shortly, and even the old 'Ages' of Stone, Bronze and Iron are being reinterpreted in social terms.

New monuments are steadily being explored and laid out, often a lengthy process; a few of these sites are not in the text but are shown on the maps since they will soon be open to visitors.

The notebooks of the first Inspector of Ancient Monuments, General Pitt Rivers, are preserved and, as well as the main working records of the Inspectorate, many files are in the Public Record Office. The photographic library of the Property Services Agency of the Department of the Environment holds the main pictorial record. Older records of state monuments are most notably in the Public Record Office, the Cottonian Collection of the British Library Manuscript Room, the King's Topographical Collection of the British Library Map Room, Hatfield House and the William Salt Library, Stafford.

Further information about each site can be found in a wide range of sources: libraries, record offices, museums, county archaeologists and local archaeological trusts all maintain files and records. The national record is the Ordnance Survey's record-cards, which give many additional references and can be consulted at the National Monuments Record, Fortress House, Savile Row, London W1. We would like to emphasize that every reader of this book will be able to make new discoveries by using his eyes and his wits: much can be dug out without using a spade.

Old Oswestry •

Moreton Corbet Castle ■

Haughmond
Abbey •
Lilleshall Abbey ■

Wroxeter •
Boscobel House ■

Acton •
Burnell Castle ■
• Buildwas
Langley
Chapel
Abbey
White Ladies
Priory ■
Wenlock
Priory ■

Mitchell's Fold •
Stone Circle, Chirbury

• Mortimer's Cross Watermill,
Lucton

Arthur's Stone, Dorstone •

• Rotherwas Chapel,
Hereford

Deerhurst •

Goodrich Castle ■
Witcombe Roman
Villa •

Hetty Pegler's
• Tump, Uley

Kings •
Wood Abbey Gatehouse

Temple Church, Bristol •

Granville Monument, •
Charlcombe
Abbey Barn, ■
Bradford
Stoney Littleton Long Barrow •
on Avon
Farleigh Castle ■

Bratton Camp and
Nunney Castle ■
White Horse ■

Glastonbury ■

Muchelney Abbey ■
Old Wardour Castle ■

Sherborne ■
Old Castle

Ninestones and
Poor Lot Barrows
Kingston Russell
Stone Circle
Maiden Castle ■

Blackbury Castle •
Southleigh
Abbotsbury Abbey ■
and St Catherine's Chapel
• Jordan
Hill Roman
Temple

Regent's Park

St James's Park and Buckingham Palace
Marlborough House

Hyde Park and
Kensington Palace
Tower of London ■

Osterley House
Apsley House
Whitehall ■
Chiswick
House ■
Lancaster House ■
Westminster
Chelsea Hospital
Palace

Kew Palace
and Gardens

Greenwich Palace and Park

Ham House ■

Richmond Park

Hampton Court and Parks

Okehampton Castle ■

Dunster •
Cleeve Abbey ■

Tintagel ■

Launceston Castle ■
Lydford ■

Prehistoric and Roman Sites

Duputh Well Chapel ■
Callington

Totnes Castle ■

Restormel Castle
Lostwithiel

Kirkham House
Paignton

Plymouth Citadel
and Harbour-Tower

St Catherine's
Castle, Fowey

Dartmouth Castle

Scilly Isles

Pendennis ■ **and**
St Mawes Castles

0   10   20   30 m
0 10 20 30 40
km

7   Historic monuments: London and the South

Ashby de la Zouche Castle

Jewry Wall, Leicester

Kirby Muxloe Castle

Lyddington
Bedehouse

Kirby Hall

Rushton
Triangular Lodge

Eleanor Cross,
Geddington

Kenilworth Castle

Chichele College

Longthorpe Tower
Peterborough

Blakeney Guildhall

Binham Priory and Cross

Creake Abbey

Baconsthorpe Castle

North Elmham Saxon Cathedral

Castle Rising

Castle Acre Priory and
Castle Gate

Cow
Tower, Norwich

Small
Houses

Caister

Greyfriars
Yarmouth

Berney Arms Windmill

Burgh Castle
Roman Fort

Weeting Castle

Grime's Graves

Warren Lodge

Thetford Priory

Isleham Priory

Bury St Edmund's
Abbey

Saxtead Green
Windmill

Leiston Abbey

Framlingham Castle

Denny Abbey

Orford Castle

Duxford Chapel

Lindsey Chapel

Houghton
House

Audley End

Mistley Towers

Wrest Park

Colchester

Hailes Abbey

Belas Knap Long Barrow

Notgrove
Long Barrow

North Leigh
Roman Villa

Minster
Lovell House

Rycote
Chapel

Berkhamsted Castle

(Verulamium)
Roman Walls

Waltham Abbey

Uffington Castle
and White Horse

Abingdon County Hall

Upnor Castle

Temple Manor

Hadleigh Castle

Rochester Castle

Waylands Smithy

The Avebury
Region

Donnington
Castle

Windsor
Castle

See inset

Tilbury
Fort

Eltham
Palace

Eynsford
Castle

Reculver

Ebbsfleet Cross

Richborough

Prehistoric Sites

Aylesford

Lullingstone
Roman Villa

Canterbury

Deal Castle and
Walmer Tower

Netheravon
Dovecot

Ludgershall Castle
and Cross

Old Soar
Manor

West Malling
Tower

Maison
Dieu

The Stonehenge
Region

Old Sarum

Farnham Castle

Dover Castle

Waverley Abbey

Horne's Place
Chapel

Dymchurch
Martello Tower

Bayham Abbey

Knowlton Circle
and Church

Bishop's Palace

Netley
Abbey

Hurstmonceaux
Castle

Portchester Castle

Titchfield Abbey

Pevensey Castle

Christchurch
Castle

Hurst
Castle

Portsmouth

Osborne House

Yarmouth Castle

Carisbrooke Castle

St Catherine's
Chapel

Appuldurcombe
House

0   10   20   30 m

0 10 20 30 40   km

Berwick on Tweed

Norham Castle

Holy Island of Lindisfarne

Dunstanburgh Castle

Warkworth Castle

Brinkburn Priory

Hadrian's Wall

Tynemouth Priory

Jarrow Monastery

Lanercost Priory

Hylton Castle

Carlisle Castle

Finchale Priory

Castle Deer-House

Penrith Castle

Mayburgh

Brougham Castle

King Arthur's Round Table

Castlerigg Stone Circle

Barnard Castle

Gisborough Priory

Whitby Abbey

Brough Castle

Egglestone Abbey

Shap Abbey

Bowes Castle

Stanwick Oppidum

Hardknot Roman Fort

Richmond Castle

Easby Abbey

Wheeldale Moor Road

Mount Grace Priory

Scarborough Castle

Middleham Castle

Rievaulx Abbey

Helmsley Castle

Byland Abbey

Furness Abbey Barrow

Fountains Abbey

Aldborough Roman Town

Kirkham Priory

Burton Agnes Manor House

Skipsea Castle

Spofforth Castle

Clifford's Tower, York Castle

Steeton Hall

Howden Church

Thornton Abbey

Monk Bretton Priory

Roche Abbey

Mattersey Priory

Peveril Castle

Bishop's Palace Lincoln

Chester Castle and Roman Amphitheatre

Bolsover Castle

Sandbach Crosses

Hardwick Old Hall

Rufford Abbey

Beeston Castle

Prehistoric Sites

Bolingbroke Castle

Croxdon Abbey

8   Historic monuments: the Midlands and the North

England

Avon

Temple Church, *Bristol* A ruin of the fourteenth or fifteenth century.

Granville Monument, *Charlcombe* A monument to Sir Bevil Granville, who was killed here at the Battle of Lansdowne in 1643.

Stoney Littleton Long Barrow One of the first of our ancient monuments, this long barrow has been in guardianship since 1884. It is sited on a low 'false crest' and tightly surrounded by barbed wire. The barrow has a long main passage with three cross-passages, was used for communal burial in Neolithic times, and was a good deal rebuilt in 1858.

Bedfordshire

Houghton House, *Ampthill* A finely sited Jacobean ruin.

Wrest Park, *Silsoe* A formal and monumental garden layout of *c.* 1700–10, later smoothed off by 'Capability' Brown and romanticized in Regency times. There is still a fine sense of enclosure, and the fabulous pavilion of 1709 must have been a rare setting for intimate receptions. The yew hedges are being replanted and the garden brought back from near-ruin. There are impressive canals dug into the heavy clay subsoil. The garden went with an older house: when this was demolished in *c.* 1840, the fine new mansion was built further away. It is now the Institute of Agricultural Engineering.

Wrest Park,
Bedfordshire: garden
pavilion

Berkshire

Donnington Castle   Only the fine turreted gateway survives of the private castle
of a fourteenth-century courtier, Sir Richard de Abberbury, who was a guardian of Richard II. The castle was largely destroyed after a twenty-month siege
in the Civil War of the 1640s.

The gate-tower led into a small courtyard which must have been closely surrounded by the domestic buildings, of which nothing can be recognized now.
The Civil War earthworks, built around the medieval castle by Colonel Boyse
in 1643–4, survive in reasonably good condition.

In the valley beneath the castle Sir Richard de Abberbury founded an almshouse which still exists.

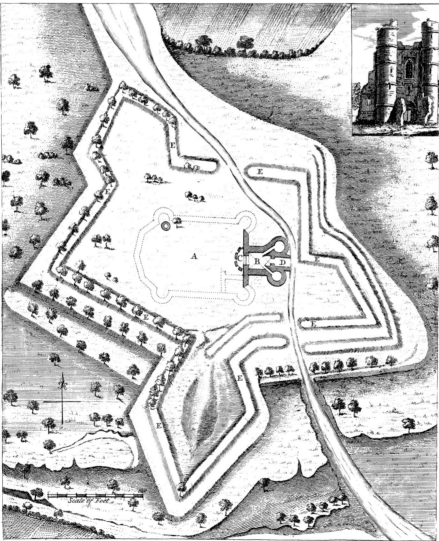

Donnington Castle,
Berkshire: engraved
plan

Donnington Castle.

A. *The Castle in Ruins*
B. *The entrance with the Towers standing*
C. *A Drinking Room erected by the Proprietor*
D. *Another Porch open at Top*
E. *Temporary Works thrown up in the Civil Wars*
* *Between the vaulted Passage* B. & *Drinking Room* C.
the Steps is a Vacancy for a Port Cullis

Windsor Castle A major royal residence and stronghold for nine centuries, Windsor, as New Windsor, was first used by Henry I to hold court in AD 1110. Old Windsor, the Saxon royal palace a couple of miles to the east, has recently been excavated, but nothing is now to be seen.

In 1167–71 Henry II rebuilt the walls of the upper bailey in stone around a palatial courtyard residence planned on the lines of Bishop Roger of Salisbury's earlier palace-castles of Sherborne (page 65) and Old Sarum (page 157). Henry III built a new princely residence in the lower bailey, the walls of which he constructed in stone. Only fragments of these early palaces remain.

Edward III spent the huge sum of £50,000 between 1350 and 1377 rebuilding the residence in the upper bailey for himself and the burnt-out ruins of Henry III's lower palace for the college of St George. St George's chapel was rebuilt on new and sumptuous lines by Edward IV in the 1470s, with the picturesque horseshoe-cloister to the west.

Although substantial fragments remain of rebuildings under Henry VIII, Elizabeth and Charles II the main impression of the visitor's tour of the state apartments is given by George IV's lavish gothic reconstruction, with a few later changes.

Cambridgeshire

Denny Abbey Remains of a church and dining-hall, later used as a barn and farm. The remains are, as usual, twelfth and fourteenth century. The first occupants were monks of Ely, then Knights Templar, then Franciscan nuns, who also owned the property of Strood (page 95).

Duxford Chapel A fourteenth-century hospital-chapel.

Isleham Priory An early Norman church of the cell or out-station of a Breton abbey, not far from the parish church.

Longthorpe Tower, Peterborough The tower of a fourteenth-century manor-house with very interesting medieval wall-paintings. (Fig. 6.)

Cheshire

Beeston Castle Beeston Castle, an extensive fortress on a commanding hilltop, was built in *c.* AD 1220–5 by the powerful Earls of Chester—close to the Welsh border, but of equal value against an English enemy. It was taken into royal hands, with the earldom, in 1237 and was kept in repair during the fourteenth century, but as a fort rather than a residential castle and only of value

as a 'long-stop' reserve in case of Welsh risings. However, it proved to be a useful stronghold in the Civil War, being well above effective cannon-fire, and was dismantled in 1646.

Chester Castle and Roman Amphitheatre   A large square tower of the once great castle can sometimes be seen. Excavation has revealed half of the large amphi-theatre of the Twentieth Legion, which was used for military training and demonstration, gladiators, hunting contests and other spectacles. Another Roman amphitheatre can be seen at Caerleon (page 192).

The whole of the historic city of Chester, with its cathedral, churches, walls, bridges and many early houses, deserves as long to explore as Canterbury or York.

Sandbach Crosses   A pair of excellent carved stone crosses, of about the ninth century AD, in a small market-place too much used for car-parking.

Beeston Castle,
Cheshire

Sandbach Crosses,
Cheshire

Cleveland

Gisborough Priory The high east end of the church of *c.* AD 1290 towers dramatically over the long one-street town and a few low walls survive among sweeping lawns, but very little else is left of this large and wealthy Augustinian priory.

Cornwall

Prehistoric and Roman Sites There are numbers of prehistoric, religious sites in Cornwall and the south-west. *Ballowall Barrow* (Carn Gluze), St Just, is a round barrow with three tomb chambers of early prehistoric date, and another barrow can be seen nearby at Tregiffian. At St Cleer the massive stones of *Trethevy Quoit* burial chamber stand up splendidly behind a row of cottages; they are not fenced off. The oval mound, however, has gone. *The Hurlers*, Minions, are three stone circles about 125 feet (35–40 metres) in diameter, set in a line in dramatic moorland country among abandoned mines. This minor sacred site can be compared with the stone circles at Avebury (page 148). On *St Breok Downs* there is a tall standing stone, and at *Carn Euny*, Sancreed, the low wall of an Iron Age hamlet, with an immense secret passage, can still be seen.

Later remains include an excavated hamlet of the Roman period, at *Chysauster*, Madron, with eight circular courtyard-houses, and *King Doniert's Stone*, St Cleer, two broken cross-bases of the ninth century AD, which stand in a neat dyked enclosure by the road.

Duputh Well-Chapel, Callington The most complete of many well-chapels in the south-west stands beside a spring which flows under the threshold, along the chapel and into a shallow basin instead of an altar. These chapels may sanctify sacred spots of pre-Christian times, or may have been used simply for baptism.

The chapel is tidily wired off beside a busy working farm.

St Catharine's Castle, Fowey A small gun-bastion of Henry VIII's reign built, with a small blockhouse on the point opposite, to protect the harbour. There is unsignposted access over the beach and up slippery cliff paths or through National Trust woods, but it is a long walk from the official car-park.

Launceston Castle A spectacular high castle-motte dominates the land round this attractive little hill-top town, which may have developed within a hill-fort of Dark Age origins. The castle was established by William the Conqueror's half-

Duputh well-chape
Cornwall

brother, Robert of Mortain, whose vast estates were concentrated in the south-west. On the motte stands a great double tower, the central ring rising high above an outer shell. It was probably built in the time of Henry III's brother, Richard, Earl of Cornwall (1227–72), who also did much work at Restormel (page 48). In the bailey, which slopes down away from the town, the north and south gates are rather incomplete and the footings of the other buildings are being painstakingly laid out, unfortunately to the detriment of the fine early Victorian landscaping.

Pendennis and St Mawes Castles A number of the wide harbour-mouths of Devon and Cornwall were protected during the fourteenth and fifteenth cen-

St Mawes Castle,
Cornwall

turies by blockhouses and forts, built by local enterprise. The town of Fowey
was sacked by the French in 1457, and Dartmouth (page 57) had been attacked
in 1404. The wide mouth of the Fal lay temptingly open to attack until
Henry VIII's great invasion scare in 1538, which led to an extensive
programme of defence works, including those at Deal (page 87), Walmer
(page 87) and Portland.

Pendennis (1539–43) was built high on the western headland, a tall round
tower within a lower sixteen-sided rampart. St Mawes (1540–3) lies closer to
the water's edge on the east side, again a round tower, but here surrounded
by three lower semi-circular bastions in clover-leaf plan. The great royal arms
carved over the entrances and the internal fittings are of fine quality; St Mawes
has elaborate Latin inscriptions carved on the bastions in praise of King Henry
VIII and his son Prince Edward as Duke of Cornwall.

These compact forts were designed to deter attacks by ship on the harbour.
When a Spanish landing party sacked Penzance in 1595 their weakness from
land-attack was made clear, and a powerful new earthwork fort was built round
the Pendennis headland in 1598–9. The value of this fort was well shown during
the Civil War, when it was held from March until August 1646 under close
siege, by the stalwart old Royalist, Colonel Arundell, who had paraded against

the Spanish Armada with Queen Elizabeth at Tilbury fifty-eight years before (page 73).

Restormel Castle
Cornwall

Restormel Castle, Lostwithiel   The castle stands on the end of a spur, looking immensely impressive as you come up to it from the south, like a great shell keep on a motte. This is all illusion: the earth out of the ditch has been piled up against the walls, as at Lydford (page 59), to give the look of a motte.

The buildings and even the defences of the bailey to the west have disappeared, and are covered in rhododendrons and lavish planting, and the 'keep' turns out to be a circular courtyard or inner bailey lined with a palatial residence. All the standing remains may be of the time of the royal Earls of Cornwall—Richard 'King of the Romans', who held the property for a few years, or his son Edmund, Earl from 1272 to 1299.

Tintagel   A spectacular promontory fort on the north Cornish coast, Tintagel is connected by legend with King Arthur. All the Dark Age or prehistoric defences have been eroded away and continuing erosion has now closed the whole peninsula.

Excavations have revealed a small late Roman farmstead and several groups of later buildings, some on terraces cut into the eastern cliffs, which may be a Dark Age monastery.

In the twelfth and thirteenth centuries there was a minor castle here, valued by its princely owners as a place to re-enact the Court of King Arthur, or, like Dunstanburgh (page 113), as an ultimate refuge. The visitor can still see two small outer wards with a gatehouse, all constructed in the time of Richard 'King of the Romans', Earl of Cornwall from 1227 to 1272. Another of his strongholds was Berkhamsted Castle (page 84).

Tintagel Castle
Cornwall

The castle was used as a prison in the fifteenth century, and abandoned in the sixteenth.

Scilly Isles   In state care on the islands there are four burial sites dating from early prehistoric times, a Roman hamlet and four gun-defences from the sixteenth and seventeenth centuries. The burial sites are all on St Mary's and all are stone-built chambers within fairly badly ruined barrows. Those at *Porth Hellick* and *Innisidgen* are in a better state, but *Bants Carn* and *Lower Innisidgen* are not so easy to make out. There are also the remains of round huts of a Roman settlement at *Bants Carn*.

On St Mary's is a Tudor fort, *Harry's Walls*, and on Tresco is *King Charles' Castle* of the mid sixteenth century, the *Old Blockhouse* of the late sixteenth century and *Cromwell's Castle* of the mid seventeenth century, all minor batteries for coastal defence.

Cumbria

Brough and Brougham Castles Two very similar castles stand 18 miles (30 km.) apart, and are difficult to remember apart. Both stand not far from the Roman and modern road, the A66, over Stainmore, both of them within Roman forts which can be seen as earthworks. Both have keeps of *c*. AD 1170 and various additions of the thirteenth and fourteenth centuries, and both were romantically rebuilt in the 1650s by Lady Anne Clifford, the last of her line. She did just the same at Appleby, halfway between the two, and also rebuilt or repaired half a dozen local churches and chapels.

Carlisle Castle Cumberland was only permanently attached to England in Henry II's reign, although William Rufus had colonized the district with English peasants and built the castle at Carlisle. Throughout the succeeding centuries, Carlisle was attacked by the Scots during incessant border warfare and sometimes captured. The Scottish allies of Parliament took Carlisle after a bitter siege in 1644–5 and the castle was held briefly by the Royalists in 1648. Even in 1745 a feeble garrison surrendered the castle to Charles Stuart, and it was recaptured by the Duke of Cumberland who used the cells to hold many of his prisoners from Culloden.

The keep is typical massive work of Henry II's time (*c*. 1160) but was much altered to serve as a gun-platform under Elizabeth. The inner bailey dates largely from the fourteenth century while the outer bailey, with its handsome nineteenth-century barrack-blocks, seems to be work of the twelfth century, much rebuilt in the thirteenth and fourteenth centuries. The keep holds the regimental museum of the Border regiment.

The full history of the city of Carlisle has not yet been revealed by excavation. It was a walled Roman town, still the centre of a district when it was given to St Cuthbert in AD 685. The colonization of 1092 seems to have had segregated quarters of the city for the English, Norman and Irish settlers, according to a late source, but the influence of the local Cumbrian and Scottish elements in the development of the town is very obscure. At the opposite end of the city a large artillery citadel was built for Henry VIII in 1541–3, then rebuilt grandiosely as Regency Assize Courts.

Castlerigg Stone Circle An irregular oval of standing stones on low ground below Skiddaw among mountainous country, clearly a local religious centre in Neolithic or Bronze Age times. (National Trust.)

Furness Abbey, Barrow Furness Abbey was second only to Fountains (page 164) among English Cistercian abbeys. It was founded in 1123 when Stephen,

later King of England, set up some monks from Savigny in Normandy near Preston, moving them here in 1127. Until they joined the Cistercians in 1147, the Savignacs were the same kind of puritanical activists. They had great estates stretching up into the Lake District and as far away as Yorkshire, and they exploited both sheep and iron. They founded six daughter houses, including Byland Abbey (page 161).

Much of the east part of the church of the twelfth century, reconstructed in the fifteenth, and the Tudor west tower still stand, making a fine ruin with the east cloister-building, a magnificent range of *c.* 1230–40. A good deal more is laid out as foundations, and the guesthouse, watercourses and so on can be seen in some detail. The infirmary-chapel is very complete and contains a site display. The sheltered valley setting, once a wilderness, is typical of the great Cistercian abbeys of the north.

Hadrian's Wall   See after Northumberland, page 118.

Hardknot Roman Fort   The usual foundations of headquarters, commandant's house, granaries, gateways, bath-house, etc., in a grim and commanding site.

King Arthur's Round Table and Mayburgh, Eamont Bridge   A pair of large religious monuments of the Neolithic or Bronze Age periods. The 'Round Table' is a fairly low open site beside the A6. Mayburgh, with a higher bank and one standing stone left, is surrounded by trees but savagely and unforgivably impinged on by the M6 and its traffic noise. The nearby Roman fort and Norman castle of Brougham (page 50) and the handsome large market-town of Penrith are successors as the focus of the district.

The Eden valley contains many more little-known early remains including *Long Meg and her daughters* 6 miles (10 km.) to the north-east and very extensive field-systems and Roman hamlets above Crosby Garrett and Crosby Ravensworth 10 miles (16 km.) to the south-east. An area of these, with proper conservation, management and skilled interpretation, would be a valuable addition to our accessible monuments.

Lanercost Priory   The monastery was founded in *c.* AD 1166 for Augustinian canons. The church, of *c.* 1220–75, is very complete, and the nave is still in use as the parish church. Of the cloister-buildings the east range is only foundations, the south range has the undercroft of the dining-hall and the west range is intact. It was converted into a house in the sixteenth century. Two fortified medieval towers, part of the gatehouse and the bridge, also survive. Scottish raids are recorded in 1296–7 and 1346.

Lanercost is beautifully sited on the Irthing between Naworth Park and Hadrian's Wall (page 118).

Penrith Castle   Remains of a foursquare late medieval castle of the 1390s, modernized in the 1470s, stand up well in a public park by the railway station.

Shap Abbey   A small abbey of the Premonstratensian order, which followed Cistercian ideals, was founded in *c.* 1201 in the remote valley of the Lowther. Of the canons, who served a number of local churches, only one is of note— Richard Redman of Levens became Bishop of St Asaph, Exeter and Ely at the end of the fifteenth century and also held the abbacy of Shap where he built the great west tower. The cloister-buildings are laid out in detail but the abbot's house is still in use as a farm, together with the farm buildings of the abbey. The Ministry's usual wire fencing is sadly in evidence.

Shap is rather like Egglestone Abbey, Durham (page 69), an even smaller and poorer house of the order.

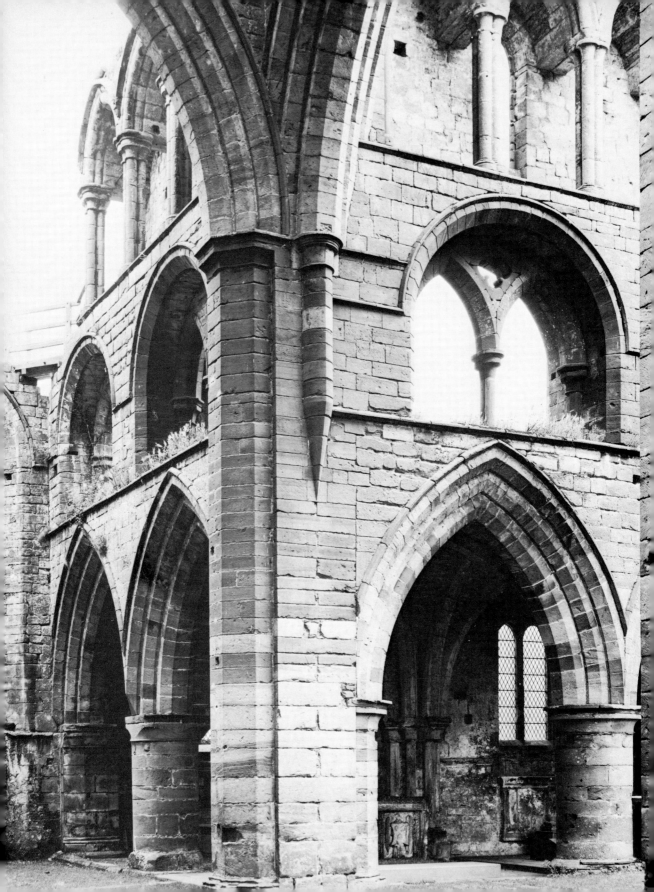

Derbyshire

Prehistoric Sites The extensive moorlands of the Low Peak around Matlock and Buxton contain very large numbers of barrows and other early sites. The bulk of the fields and farms must always have been in the valleys as they are today. This is a very good area to study the ridge-and-furrow and lynchets of the medieval field-systems; most of the outlines and perhaps many of the details of these fields may go back to Roman and prehistoric times. They form a 'corduroy' pattern on old pasture fields, especially in morning and evening light, and are a sign of ploughing.

As a whole the moors are a nineteenth-century landscape with square fields, low farms and abandoned mines. *Arbor Low*, a local 'stonehenge' with something between forty-six and fifty-nine stones all flat on the ground, and two opposed entrances through an outer bank, lies in this sort of area. There is a barrow set into the outer bank and another 350 yards (300 metres) away. Not far past this the straight line of the *Roman road* from Buxton to Littlechester (near Derby) can be picked out. Also nearby was an important Saxon chief's burial at *Benty Grange*. Finds from Arbor Low are in the British Museum and Sheffield and Buxton Museums.

On Stanton Moor, 6 miles (10 km.) to the east, the *Nine Ladies* stone circle survives from a group of at least four circles in a more authentic setting of open rough pasture among seventy barrows. The whole moor deserves careful management and control; the eastern slope is National Trust land.

Hob Hurst's House, Beeley, is a barrow with its outer bank on the moors east of Chatsworth Park, and another stone circle and barrow are on *Eyam Moor*. All are quite difficult to get to.

Bolsover Castle The castle is magnificently placed on a sheer promontory, overlooking industrial sprawl and the edges of Sheffield, an ideal site for a prehistoric stronghold.

The derelict castle was transformed by Charles Cavendish who built a new keep, the Little Castle, in 1612–16 as a romantic fantasy in a dream of chivalry. His mother, Bess of Hardwick, built her own superb Elizabethan mansion which stands dramatically in sight through the murk a few miles away. She built Hardwick in the 1590s when she was over seventy and must have had as her designer the great Elizabethan architect Robert Smythson. Smythson (who died in 1614), his son John (who died in 1634) and his grandson Huntingdon (who died in 1648) all contributed to Bolsover for Bess's son Charles (who died in 1617) and grandson William, Duke of Newcastle (who died in 1676). The great mansion which they built on to the sham castle now stands round the Great Court, roofless since it was abandoned in the eighteenth century. In the Duke's lifetime it was built and rebuilt, fortified and surrendered, sold for demolition, rescued and reroofed. It shows many signs of this complex building history, but all is of the seventeenth century.

Bolsover has a unique character. The vast state rooms open to the sky contrast vividly with the tiny ornate rooms of the Little Castle which still have wall-paintings, panelling, vaulting and astonishing fireplaces. Medieval and classical details and shapes combine and clash. The fireplaces were lifted from an Italian textbook on architecture; the keep must have been based on the earlier 'dream-keep' of the Percies at Warkworth in Northumberland (page 116); the exploded pediments of the long gallery windows are stolen from Flemish baroque, but between them the wild rusticated pilasters are like nothing in Europe.

The approach by a fine avenue across the outer court, the magnificent riding school, the great terrace and the well-kept fountain garden contribute to the powerful character and give some idea of the setting of a great house of the seventeenth century.

Hardwick Old Hall Elizabeth Hardwick, Mistress Barley, Lady Cavendish, Lady St Loe, the Countess of Shrewsbury as 'Bess of Hardwick' was named in her long life, celebrated her harassed fourth husband's death by setting out to build, with his money, the 'supreme triumph of Elizabethan architecture'. At her birthplace, Hardwick, in 1590–7 she built the ruthless and romantic house which is now one of the best known of National Trust properties.

A hundred yards away is the shell of her father's house, which she had bought from her brother in 1570. She rebuilt it in 1587–9 on a vast scale four to six storeys high. This indomitable, proud, furious, selfish and unyielding woman was already in her late sixties and separated from her husband.

The inside of the older house has collapsed, but a good deal of lavish plaster-work remains and we can see the layout of the big reception rooms at the top of the house with a staircase tower foreshadowing the six great towers of the new house. The Hunting Tower in the grounds was built with the old house. Part of the grounds is now a country park.

Peveril Castle, Castleton The dominating and well-preserved stronghold was the more-or-less private fortress of William the Conqueror's local bailiff, William Peveril. He simply walled round the precipitous rocky projection. In royal hands again in 1173–4 the castle was strengthened with a keep where the natural defences were weakest. Of Henry II's keeps Peveril is very much the baby of the family; it is about 35 feet (11 metres) square, compared to 55 feet (17 metres) at Scarborough (page 169) and about 115 feet (35 metres) at Dover (page 87). It cost about £200 whereas Dover cost £4,000. The castle was steadily repaired for as long as the northern barons were politically unreli-

able, and then given away to favourites or queens. The castle has been among the lands of the Duchy of Lancaster since 1372.

The role of the castle and the whole estate in developing the lead mines of the area deserves study. Below the castle the vast Peak Cavern has long been a showplace.

Devon

Blackbury Castle, Southleigh   A well-preserved hill-fort on a long narrow ridge, very pleasantly set in open woodland.

Dartmouth Castle   The town of Dartmouth developed at the mouth of the Dart, and reduced the importance of Totnes (page 61), 7 miles (12 km.) upstream at the head of the estuary. Totnes remained a local market-town and Dartmouth became a great trading centre for Bordeaux wine and Newfoundland cod, receiving a charter in 1341.

Below the town on a headland looking out to sea was a chapel of St Petrox, possibly of early Christian origin, and built to mark the harbour-mouth. Round the chapel the townsmen built or rebuilt a castle in 1374–88 with a large outer ward climbing the hillside and a small inner ward on the point around the chapel.

The large round tower at the seaward point of the inner ward was strengthened by a low gun-bastion built out to command the harbour-mouth in 1481. This seems to be the first work in the country designed specifically for artillery and can be compared with similar low barbicans built at Rhodes. The bastion seems to have been heightened in 1494 and again in Elizabethan times. The chapel was rebuilt as a large parish church in late Gothic style in 1641, abolishing the defences of the inner ward. The seaward tower of the outer ward was rebuilt as a gun-battery in 1545, 1690, 1747 and again in 1861, but the large town-castle had shrunk to a coastal battery by this time, remaining 'on the books' until 1955. It seems to have been taken over by the state in 1660.

A chain could be stretched across the harbour-mouth to stop ships, and Kingswear Castle, another round tower with a gun-battery in front, was built or rebuilt in 1491. Upstream from Dartmouth Castle, at the south end of the town, is another battery at Bayard's Cove dating from 1509–10, or perhaps 1535, of a characteristic flat-fronted round-ended design briefly fashionable in European defences at about this time.

Dartmouth and Kingswear were strengthened by the Royalists in the Civil War with powerful earthwork forts stretching uphill on both sides of the river, but were taken by Fairfax without much trouble in 1646.

Dartmouth is very popular with visitors, but has kept its magic. Saturday morning is a surprisingly good time to visit the castle, when many holiday-makers are travelling home or arriving.

Hound Tor, Manaton   On the edge of Dartmoor lie the remains of a medieval hamlet used for summer grazing: the low stone walls are capped by turf.

Lydford   This charming little grey village lies within the massive ramparts of a Saxon fortress-town, which was once far more populous and important. The Normans destroyed forty houses to clear room for a castle in the north-west quarter of the town. In the far corner, perched up on the edge of a ravine beyond the church, are the powerful earthworks of a little early Norman fort. East of the church lie the more massive earthworks of the castle, with a bailey running north from a stumpy little Norman keep. The keep was raised by a floor in the thirteenth century and had earth piled round the ground floor to make it seem to stand on a motte, a trick used also at Restormel (page 48). Even this does not make the castle very impressive, and it does not feel much of a strongpoint since it is commanded by hills all round, despite the spectacular ravine.

The pleasant little church of St Petroc was built perhaps in the seventh century, sacked by Vikings in AD 997 and was probably incorporated in the first stage of the Norman castle, later left out of a reduced defence. As a local centre Lydford was replaced by Okehampton (page 60) by the thirteenth century.

The DoE propose to maintain the whole north-west quarter of the Saxon town as open ground.

Okehampton Castle Okehampton Castle lies right away from the town on a most attractive and picturesque site with even less outlook than Lydford. It has much more the feel of a hunting-lodge and it is hard to believe that this was ever a serious castle. The Norman castle was probably at the centre of the town near the crossings of the two Okement rivers, abandoned for this site by the Courtenay Earls of Devon in about AD 1300. The present remains all seem to be of fourteenth-century date and consist of a large manor-house slightly

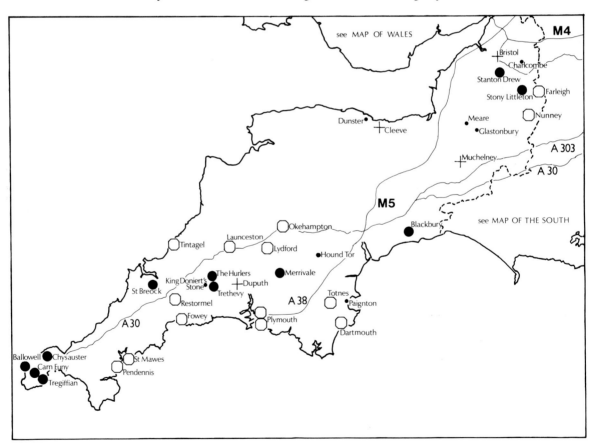

squashed round a narrow courtyard on a low ridge, with a tower-house, like a keep, on a high spur above.

The castle was excavated and consolidated privately in 1911–13, and maintained by a private trust from 1917 until 1967 when it was placed in Guardianship.

Kirkham House, Paignton   This was probably a chantry-priest's house of *c.* AD 1500, rather heavily restored and set in one of the less attractive suburbs of Torbay. The Borough Public Works Depot looms over it in brutish taste.

Behind the very fine parish church are remains of the Bishop of Exeter's palace, a corner tower and two long battlemented walls.

Plymouth Citadel and Harbour-Tower   A fort of 1666–70 designed by Sir Bernard de Gomme and very like his Tilbury Fort (page 73), except that the outer earthworks have been levelled. The Royal Marine Commandos run guided tours in the afternoon, and make visitors feel welcome.

Map of the south-est of England. (See :y on Map 1 for pes of monument)

The tower of 1665 on Mount Batten island can sometimes be visited.

Totnes Castle   At the head of the great estuary of the Dart, Totnes was a fortified late Saxon town. A fine large motte-and-bailey castle was forced into the town by the Normans, just as at Launceston (page 44).

The main buildings in the bailey have gone, covered with fine turf and well-grown trees, and the motte is crowned with a well-preserved shell keep, the size of Launceston but lacking the high tower. From the keep there are very fine views of the church and slate roofs of the handsome little town, of the wonderful wooded hills, the broad silver streak of the Dart and the high peaks of Dartmoor. From the fourteenth century the de la Zouches had more interest in the income from the land than in the castle, and there are no later remains here. At the other end of the estuary, however, new defences at Dartmouth (page 57) effectively replaced Totnes Castle, and much of the trade of the town also passed to Dartmouth, another fine town, which should always be visited with Totnes. (Fig. 5.)

Dorset

Abbotsbury Abbey and St Catherine's Chapel   A gable of one of the minor buildings and a hill-top chapel with a beacon tower are the DoE remains. The visitor can also note an overgrown foundation of the abbey church in the present churchyard, remains of the gatehouse in the lane just south-west of the churchyard, a magnificent roofless abbey-barn, and visit the famous swannery.

61

Christchurch Castle Of the castle of the Earls of Devon there remains a motte with a tower of the fourteenth century. The shops at the central crossroads of the once small town back onto this with pleasant incongruity. Cut off by a high fence is a Norman house, now roofless, which must have stood within the bailey and been the lodging of the constable of the castle.

Jordan Hill Roman Temple, Preston A few fragments remain, well wired off from the fine surrounding country, above a large holiday camp.

Kingston Russell Stone Circle On a high ridge eighteen fallen stones lie round in a rough sort of circle about 80 feet (23 metres) in diameter, perhaps remains of a prehistoric homestead, barrow or stone circle. On the long mile walk back a ruined long barrow shows over a hedge.

Knowlton Circle and Church A ruined Norman church in the centre of a middle-sized prehistoric henge-monument 3,000 years older. Many other prehistoric barrows and henges cluster round, but most are levelled and show only on aerial photographs. This important group of ancient sacred sites deserves more attention and less wire. Does the church really signify that this was always recognized as a sacred spot? Where, too, was the medieval village?

Maiden Castle Well before the great Iron Age hill-fort, the eastern hill was surrounded by a Neolithic camp, and later an immensely long mound or barrow was piled up, presumably as a burial monument. The hill-fort was excavated in 1934–8. Its long and complicated development over perhaps four or five centuries made this the most imposing fortress in the country, the tribal capital of the Durotriges, with three vast ramparts enclosing about 20 hectares.

The hill-top has far too much wiring and fencing: it should be grazed only by sheep and not by cattle, who are causing substantial erosion. People, too, are damaging Maiden Castle simply by walking and some ineffectual wire barriers make this worse.

The eastern entrance looks down on the peaceful expanse of Dorset farmland. The excavations discovered a dramatic story here. The dismantled gates, the defenders buried close by where they fell, one with a heavy catapult arrow in his spine, make it clear that the Roman conquest was violent. The Second Legion stormed the gate with linked shields under cover of a heavy ballista bombardment.

We do not fully know how the native population was transferred to the lowland town of Dorchester close by in the first century AD. Nor do we know why a Roman temple, which can be seen as foundations behind a fence, was built

63

Plate IX

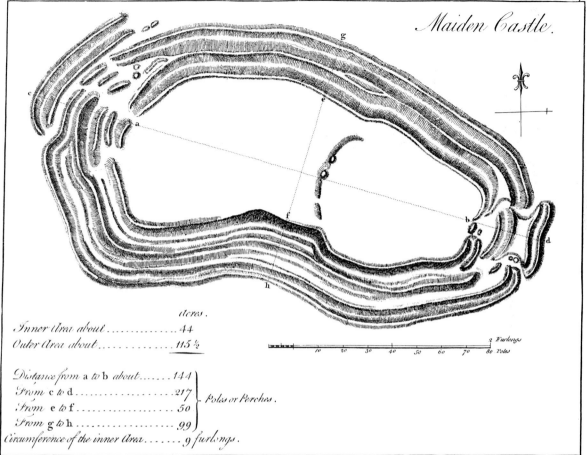

Maiden Castle.

	acres.
Inner Area about	44
Outer Area about	115 ½

Distance from a to b about	144
From c to d	217
From e to f	50
From g to h	99
Circumference of the inner Area	9 furlongs.

Poles or Perches.

Above left
Christchurch Castle,
Dorset

Left
Knowlton Church and
prehistoric monument,
Dorset

Above
Maiden Castle,
Dorset, from an
engraving

within the fortress in the fourth century. Visitors should remember to bring extra sweaters and kites.

The finds can be seen in Dorchester Museum, but the town has not very much to see. Just outside Dorchester, on the south, is Maumbury, a fine prehistoric henge-monument, scooped out by the Romans to make an amphitheatre and used as a fort in the Civil War of the 1640s. It is surrounded by one of the older suburbs of Dorchester and a ring of trees. (Fig. 4.)

Sherborne Old Castle   The castle stands on a broad rise away to the east of the handsome town of Sherborne. It was built by the greatest magnate of his day, Roger, Bishop of Salisbury (1103–39), who often acted as Regent while Henry I was in Normandy.

The castle has a large octagonal outer ward. Most of the defences have gone, including the main gate to the north, but the magnificent south-west gate stands

four storeys high and now forms the entrance. In the centre of the castle lie the palatial buildings of Roger's inner ward. They are grouped regularly round a square of courtyard as in his other great castle at Old Sarum (page 157), or as in Wolvesey Castle at Winchester, but quite unlike any ordinary domestic or even royal buildings of the period.

The buildings survive as high masses of shapeless flint, with a little of the fine and elaborate carving left in places. As at Old Sarum a massive tower or keep was incorporated in one corner of the courtyard, but it is not easy to make out anything more about the original use of the lofty rooms, and excavation is still proceeding.

The castle was in royal hands from 1135 to 1354, and was owned by Sir Walter Raleigh from 1592. He seems to have started to modernize it, but soon moved to a new lodge in the park, which now forms the core of Sherborne Castle. The Old Castle, like so many others, was held for the King in the Civil War, stormed, dismantled and abandoned. A fine bastion, added at this time, lies outside the ditch just north of the entrance to the castle.

Winterborne Abbas Ninestones and Poor Lot Barrows   Two tall and seven small stones stand in a neat iron-fenced enclosure on a fast main road with no layby. There are fine overshadowing beech trees and a very Regency look to it all. Is this a real prehistoric stone circle, or the ruins of a robbed barrow of the Bronze Age, or a jolly fake?

Further west on Poor Lot a good number of barrows still survive recent ploughing. There are plenty to admire and study, though it is not very clear which are the 'official' ones.

Durham

Barnard Castle   Bernard de Baliol built a castle in *c.* AD 1100 on a high cliff on the River Tees, just below where the narrow dale opens out from the Pennine moors into the high farming land of south Durham. The castles of Pickering and Helmsley (page 166) mark the edge of the Yorkshire moors in a very similar way. His family have left their memory and the name of the small north French town of Bailleul stamped firmly in ways that few can match. Guy de Baliol, father of Bernard, came over with William the Conqueror, not as a Norman baron but as an ally from the neighbouring territory of Picardy. He was rewarded with great estates in the Midlands. John de Baliol, four generations later, married the Scottish heiress of Galloway, was Regent of Scotland and founded the Oxford college which still bears his name, well known for Scots and learning. His son John was crowned King of Scotland in 1292 but lost the throne and his English estates to the domineering Edward I. The Bishops of Durham seized the castle, which they had often claimed, but Edward I, resenting yet another overmighty subject, handed it to the Earls of Warwick. Most of the spectacular standing remains date from the time of the Bishops and the Earls.

The castle, the fine town and the whole lordship are very rewarding to study and there are many interesting problems. Was this a prehistoric or Dark Age fortress? Was the town at first inside the defences? And the market outside? How did the park, the home farm and the hamlets fit together?

Barnard Castle never suffered more than a few minor sieges, the last in the reckless and tragic Northern Rising of 1569 which the Queen's steward George

Bowes delayed for a crucial few days. His family, which came from Bowes (page 68) only 4 miles (6 km.) away, have also left an honoured name. Their mansions at Streatlam and Gibside (where the fine Georgian chapel is cared for by the National Trust) are in ruins; but the fine collections of the Bowes Museum give Barnard Castle a strong French flavour, as it must have had in the days of the Baliols.

Castle Deer-House, Bishop Auckland   A Georgian deer-shelter in the Bishop of Durham's park.

Bowes Castle   Within a Roman fort high up on the River Greta the Breton Earls of Richmond established an outpost-fort on the Roman road across the Pennines that we know as the A66(T). Cumbria was quite often part of Scotland until Henry II took it for good in 1157, and at these times Bowes was very much a frontier fort. Henry II held Bowes during the Richmond succession and we have his records of £571 spent on the castle between 1171 and 1187. His dour rectangular keep built at this time is a good deal bigger than Newcastle

Finchale Priory,
Co. Durham

and Carlisle (page 50), and should also be compared with Brougham and Brough (page 50). Earthworks of the castle outer wards can be seen.

Egglestone Abbey In a quiet setting not far from the Tees lie the remains of a poor house of the strict Premonstratensian canons, founded in 1189. The chancel and nave of the church are fairly complete, and the ruins can be compared with Shap (page 53) and Easby (page 164) of the same order.

Finchale Priory Godric, an entrepreneur in Spanish exports, set up as a hermit here in a low gentle loop of the Wear only 3 miles (5 km.) from the tremendous sweep of the river at Durham. He probably took to it in AD 1130–40 when there was a civil war and a lot of people went into religion. Godric always exaggerated both his age and how long he had been there, and by the time he died in 1170 he claimed he was 105 and had been there for sixty years. In no time he was a saint and a monastery was founded here in the minor religious boom of the 1190s. The monks of Durham made a successful takeover bid and ran the place as a holiday hostel for themselves.

69

The thirteenth- and fourteenth-century buildings are fairly complete, but are not yet fully understood.

This beautiful site is suffering the worst kind of commercial exploitation, with a camp site alongside and a caravan site on the brow of the hill above. Spiky railings go right round and cut you off a few feet short of the river. A far wider area should be in public hands, and it should be managed by people who can display and interpret much visited tourist sites. The bright cream shacks should be hacked down and the lurid pink zig-zag paths with their concrete edging should be rooted out. But perhaps Godric feels at home with all this.

Essex

Audley End   This great mansion is the only large country house in the care of the Department of the Environment. Mansions which have become national property have generally been transferred to the National Trust.

Audley End was built in the reign of James I (between 1603 and 1616) by the Earl of Suffolk on the site of the Benedictine abbey of Walden which was converted into a residence after the dissolution. In 1669 Charles II bought the house to serve as a royal palace and it was sold back to the family in 1701. In 1721 three sides of the great outer court were demolished and so in 1749 was one side of the main inner courtyard. Extensive repairs and adaptations were undertaken by the first Lord Braybrooke in 1765–97. He fitted up the chapel in 'Strawberry Hill Gothick' and had a suite of rooms on the ground floor of the south wing designed by Robert Adam, in the fashionable style of the day. But his external repairs to the house followed the lines of the Jacobean design.

Almost every detail of the interior of the house, however, dates from the third Lord Braybrooke's time, and is an extraordinarily rich Regency version of the Jacobean style. Throughout the house there are many fine fittings and furnishings of the eighteenth and nineteenth centuries. The house stands in extensive grounds, laid out by 'Capability' Brown in 1763 and later years. A number of temples and columns commemorate the end of the seven years war, George III's recovery from insanity and so on. The large Jacobean stables are soon to be opened as a museum of agriculture.

Colchester   A section of the massive *Lexden Earthworks*, stretching away around *Camulodunum*, tribal capital of the Catuvellauni, can be seen. At *St Botolph's Priory* the ruined nave of the church of an Augustinian monastery remains, with the early Norman arches made of Roman brick looted from the town. The gateway of the Benedictine *St John's Abbey* has fine flintwork.

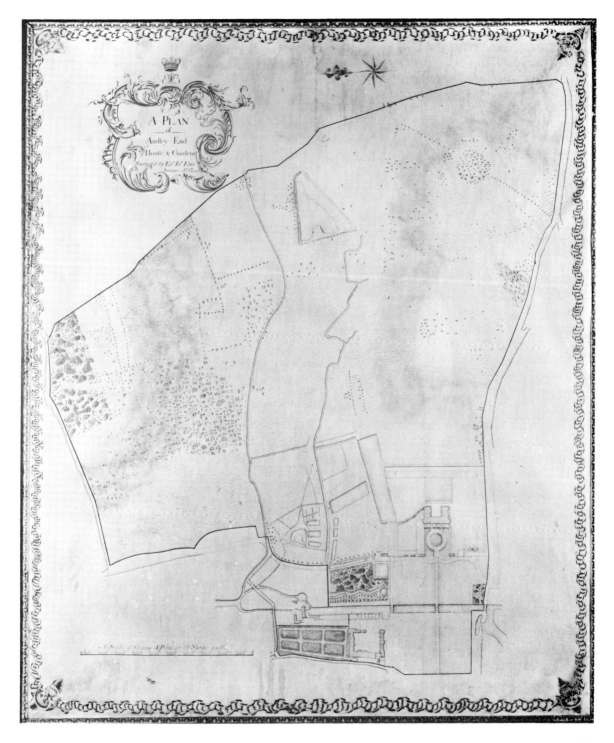

A PLAN
of
Audley End
House & Gardens

71

Hadleigh Castle Overlooking the Thames estuary behind Canvey Island, the
castle was built in *c.* AD 1230 as a semi-official contribution to national defence
on a coast which must always have seemed dangerously open to coastal raids.
Hubert de Burgh, a powerful royal servant under John and Henry III, also
held the 'three castles' in upper Gwent, rebuilding Grosmont and Skenfrith
(page 197), and he overhauled Dover (page 87).

The main wall surrounds a rough oval, and is not as impressive as Constable
painted it. At first it had small square towers projecting no more than the
Bigod's work of *c.* 1180–90 at Framlingham (page 139), of which de Burgh was
guardian at about this time. It is odd that such a distinguished expert, who
had held both Chinon in Touraine and Dover in memorable sieges, did not
insist on the characteristic round, solid-backed towers of his Gwent castles or
the distinctive pointed curves of his Dover towers. Most of the towers were
rebuilt in 1361–70 in a passing enthusiasm of Edward III's for coastal defence.
He spent £2,300 on the castle.

Extensive excavation of about a quarter of the castle in 1971–2 revealed
much of interest. The plan of the main apartments of *c.* 1300, when the castle

was in the Queen's hands, was recovered with many details of their demolition in the 1550s when the castle was sold off by the Crown. Objects recovered included pottery, coins, floor-tiles, horse-shoes, keys and arrow-heads.

Two very interesting groups of bones have been studied, one from about the late thirteenth century when the castle was a rather neglected royal fortress, one from approximately 1500 when the occupants and status of the castle are not clear: the whole estate was passing rapidly from hand to hand in court circles. In the early period the constable, it may be suggested, was enjoying chops and steak in his private room, with some mutton, pork, venison, whelks, oysters, cockles and mussels. At the later time, the bailiff's family may have preferred mutton and were eating cod, whiting, flounder and crab. At both times chicken, dove, goose, duck, rabbit, hare and pheasant were present. The venison may have come from the park, documented in *c.* 1310. The later bailiff or occupant seems also, from the bone evidence, to have kept for sport a young ferret and a merlin, while many wild birds and small rodents are also represented.

This kind of information is a great advance, and there is still more to learn about the castle's relation to the whole estate, with its barns, granges, vineyards, mills, wharves, and the park with its hunting-lodge. The name Hadleigh, the 'heather-clearing', suggests that woodland and hunting were always important here.

The little Norman church, lost among suburban sprawl, has fine wall-paintings from the castle's royal days.

Mistley Towers The plain church (AD 1735) of a Georgian 'new town' was embellished in 1776 with porticoes and a pair of domed towers, designed by Robert Adam. Only the towers are left.

Tilbury Fort On the site of one of Henry VIII's coastal battery-towers, where Elizabeth reviewed her forces against an Armada landing in 1588, a fort was built in 1670–83 following the shock and disgrace of the Dutch raid on the Medway in 1667 (page 95). While it was being built, the Chief Engineer, Sir Bernard de Gomme, for some reason missed off the most important part, the bastion projecting into and commanding the Thames. The fort has most of its outer ditches and earthworks, which de Gomme's similar Plymouth citadel (page 61) has lost.

There is an amazing variety of later gun-emplacements especially of 1868 and *c.* 1910, but the only action the fort ever saw was shooting down an airship in the First World War.

Waltham Abbey Gatehouse, Entry and Bridge In expiation of Thomas Becket's murder Henry II reconstructed Harold's church at Waltham on a vast scale

and refounded it as an Augustinian abbey in AD 1177. The older nave of *c.* 1100 is now the parish church. The entry on the north of the cloister-buildings is all that is left of Henry II's work. The gatehouse and bridge leading to it are of fourteenth-century date.

Gloucestershire

Belas Knap Long Barrow, Charlton Abbots   A very complete Neolithic burial mound. At the wider 'entrance' end is a very fine dummy entrance, set back, but the burial chambers themselves are set in the sides. In the four chambers, dug into in 1863–5, remains of thirty-eight individuals have been found, but it is uncertain whether they come from one leading family or a whole community and our ideas on population and settlement in this period are very varied.

Deerhurst   Across the road from the very fine and important Anglo-Saxon parish church is a small chapel, built into one wing of the Jacobean priory court farm. It is one of the most precisely dated of early churches since a fine inscription was found in the garden in the seventeenth century. It has been preserved ever since in the Ashmolean Museum at Oxford and may be translated:

> Earl Odda ordered this Royal Hall to be built and dedicated in honour of the Holy Trinity for the soul of his brother Aelfric which was taken in this place. Ealdred was the Bishop who dedicated it on the second of the Ides of April in the fourteenth year of the reign of Edward King of the English.

Few early buildings are as well dated as this, opened for worship on 12 April 1056. Research is now in progress on all the archaeological and architectural, political and religious, economic and social aspects of Deerhurst. The landscape is being studied as a whole, and the buildings analysed in wide-ranging ways.

We know that there was a religious house established here quite early in the Saxon period, and it is astonishing that two of its major buildings survive. Earl Odda, who also died in 1056, was an eminent nobleman, perhaps a relative of Edward the Confessor, who cannot have liked him much since he commandeered Deerhurst in 1059, and split the property in half between Westminster and St Denis, the two great royal churches just outside London and Paris.

The Odda chapel was on the larger part which went to Westminster and was sold by the Church only ten years ago. The main church went to St Denis and this estate was treated as a commercial investment with three or four monks out-stationed to supervise the exploitation of the estate. Every penny went to France and the Saxon church was not rebuilt. We are only beginning to understand how economic factors like this have affected the architecture.

The Bishop who consecrated the 'Royal Hall' or memorial chapel, Ealdred, is well known as the adroit Archbishop of York who crowned both Harold on 6 January 1066 and William the Conqueror on Christmas Day the same year.

This long-term and detailed research is being regularly reported on and sets a fine example of what can be done economically and imaginatively around many other monuments. We will soon begin to understand why there are two churches: a 'family' of churches is sometimes found, as at Canterbury (page 86). All the first-floor doorways in the main church show that it was ringed with upper chambers or galleries: what were they for? How did the hamlets on the estate and their fields work together? As we see Deerhurst in a larger and truer perspective we will be learning more, not only about other places, but about the very basis of our society.

...ORIBVS · CAESARIBVS
...NTONINO · AVG · TRIBVNICIAE
...TESTATIS · XVII · COS · III · ET · L · AVR
ELIO · VERO · AVG · ARMENIACO · TRIB
VNICIAE · POTESTATIS · III · COS · II
VEXILLATIO · LEG · XX · VV · FECIT · SVB · CVRA
SEXTI · CALPVRNI · AGRICOLAE
LEGATI · AVGVSTORVM · PR · PR

Building inscriptions
(*top*) Roman from
Corbridge
(page 121)
(*centre*) Anglo-
Saxon from
Deerhurst
(*bottom*) Elizabethan
from Old Wardour
(page 157)

GENTIS ARVNDELLÆ THOMAS LANHERNIA PROLES
IVNIOR · HOC MERVIT PRIMA SEDERE LOCO ·
VT SEDIT CECIDIT · SINE CRIMINE PLECTITVR ILLE
INSONS · INSONTEM FATA SEQVVTA PROBANT ·
NAM QVÆ PATRIS ERANT MATTHÆVS FILIVS EMIT
EMPTA AVXIT · STVDIO PRINCIPIS AVCTA MANENT
COMPRECOR AVCTA DIV MANEANT AVGENDA PER ÆVVM
HÆC DEDIT · ERIPVIT · RESTITVITQVE DEVS
1578

Hailes Abbey The Cistercian abbey was founded in 1246 by King Henry III's brother, Richard, Earl of Cornwall and 'King of the Romans', and dedicated in 1251. The ruins were gradually destroyed except for parts of the cloister walls: Following extensive excavations in Victorian times the church was laid out in trees, a unique evocation of the building.

Hailes became a great pilgrimage centre with a guaranteed phial of the Holy Blood venerated in a shrine behind the high altar, surrounded by an exotic apse with apsidal chapels, probably copied from Croxden Abbey in Staffordshire (page 136). The royal Earls of Cornwall also held Tintagel (page 48) and Berkhamsted (page 84).

Kings Wood Abbey Gatehouse The fourteenth-century gatehouse of a twelfth-century Cistercian abbey.

Notgrove Long Barrow A group of five badly ruined Neolithic burial chambers set round a central passage. The mound has been robbed away and excavations have revealed some burials and finds which are at Cheltenham Museum.

Hetty Pegler's Tump, Uley A fairly complete long barrow, again with five chambers and a central passage, all much dug into in the nineteenth century. The old county of Gloucestershire contains at least fifty long barrows, all on fairly high ground. Many more in lower and more fertile terrain must have been destroyed by cultivation long ago. Most of the ones we know were preserved in open downland pasture only enclosed and broken up for farming in *c.* 1780–1840.

Witcombe Roman Villa Three rooms with mosaic floors remain in the bath suite of this grand country house. It was cleared in 1818, but is almost all covered now.

Hampshire

Bishops' Waltham Palace The tall flint ruins of a large palace of the Bishops of Winchester, of the twelfth century but much rebuilt in the fifteenth. These large residences planned compactly round a courtyard can be seen in Henry of Blois' other work, Wolvesy palace at Winchester, and at Roger of Salisbury's strongholds of Sherborne (page 65) and Old Sarum (page 157). Royal palaces were seldom as grand or as comfortable.

The palace has been sliced off from the pleasant little town by a wide new main road.

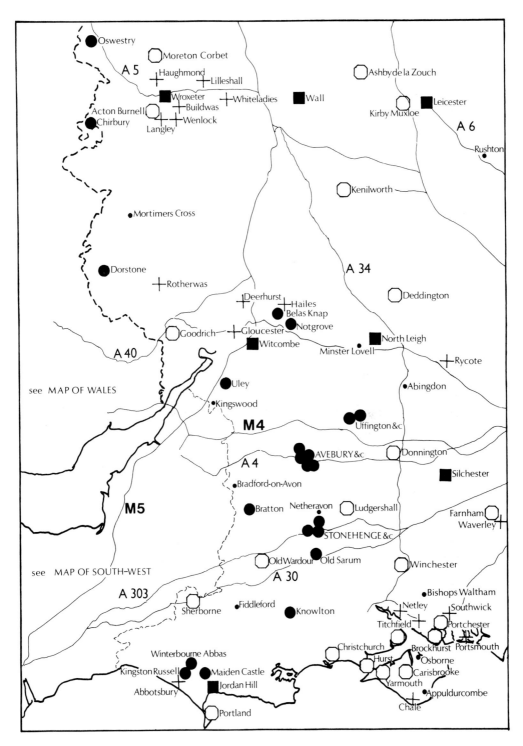

10   Map of the south of England. (See key on Map 1 for types of monument)

Netley Abbey,
Hampshire

Hurst Castle On a shingle bank in the Solent Henry VIII's engineers built
a fort in 1541–4, as usual a complicated central-planned job. The Venetians,
trendsetters in fortress-building, had a vogue for these fifty years earlier, but
by this time were building proper gun-bastions. At either end of Europe the
Turks and the English were building these elaborate, hopelessly out of date
little forts. Long side wings were added in 1873.

Netley Abbey   The abbey was founded in 1239, one of a small number of Cistercian houses (including Hailes, page 77) which owe their origin to the spasmodic religious enthusiasm of the thirteenth century. The enthusiast here was the French knight turned Bishop of Winchester, Peter des Roches. As guardian to the young Henry III he was involved in a memorable struggle with Hubert de Burgh of Hadleigh (page 72) and the 'three castles' (page 197). He had a good deal on his conscience and also founded Titchfield Abbey (page 82). A good deal remains of the lower walls of the church and of the cloister-buildings. The abbey was incorporated into the mansion of the Paulet Marquesses of Winchester but unroofed, abandoned and robbed in about 1700. The ruins in their dramatic site on the Solent attracted early tourists such as Horace Walpole and Thomas Gray, but are now a great deal trimmer and better maintained. (Fig. 3.)

Portchester Castle   This Roman fort whose walls still stand very nearly complete was built a few years before AD 300, perhaps in the time of Carausius, who maintained himself as an independent emperor in Britain between AD 286 and 293. No permanent stone buildings have been found, but recent excavations have revealed a very important sequence of Anglo-Saxon occupation with many rubbish pits, some small sunken huts and a few small rectangular buildings. It is not clear how far they were Roman dependants or invaders. Later in Saxon times, in the tenth and eleventh centuries, there were groups of buildings whose changes and rebuilding have been revealed in excavation. In Norman times one Roman corner tower was replaced by a massive Norman keep and the bailey of the castle was formed by cutting off a section of the old fort by a ditch across the inside. In the opposite, south-eastern corner, a Norman church was built, probably on an earlier site. This was occupied for a time between 1133 and about 1150 by the priory of Augustinian canons founded by Henry I.

Portsmouth Garrison Church   A hospital of AD 1212, built on the lines of a church. The ruined nave was the ward, for travellers and the sick; the chancel, which is still roofed, was the chapel. It was much restored in 1866.

Portsmouth Landport and King James Gate   As the harbours of the Cinque Ports silted up, the value of Portsmouth harbour as a naval base grew. The town was established, perhaps at a stroke in 1194 by King Richard the Lionheart, and protected by ramparts 200 years later. Successive governments from 1400 to 1950 have lavished more cash on defending Portsmouth than anywhere in the country, none ever realizing or admitting that if the navy had failed to stop an invader, it was certainly too late to protect it.

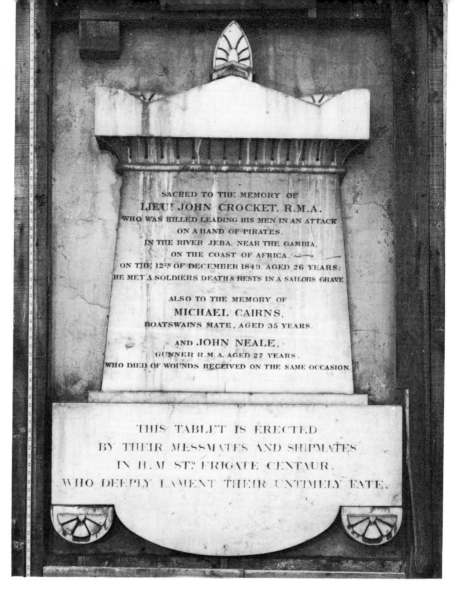

SACRED TO THE MEMORY OF
LIEU? JOHN CROCKET, R.M.A.
WHO WAS KILLED LEADING HIS MEN IN AN ATTACK
ON A BAND OF PIRATES,
IN THE RIVER JEBA, NEAR THE GAMBIA,
ON THE COAST OF AFRICA,——
ON THE 12ᵀᴴ OF DECEMBER 1849, AGED 26 YEARS,
HE MET A SOLDIERS DEATH & RESTS IN A SAILORS GRAVE

ALSO TO THE MEMORY OF
MICHAEL CAIRNS,
BOATSWAINS MATE, AGED 35 YEARS.

AND JOHN NEALE,
GUNNER R.M.A. AGED 27 YEARS,
WHO DIED OF WOUNDS RECEIVED ON THE SAME OCCASION.

THIS TABLET IS ERECTED
BY THEIR MESSMATES AND SHIPMATES
IN H.M. ST? FRIGATE CENTAUR,
WHO DEEPLY LAMENT THEIR UNTIMELY FATE.

Some of these defences exist; some are still naval or military. The seaward
defences of the town are in a fair state as a public walk. Portsmouth Museum
runs the Round Tower and Southsea Castle and the DoE maintain two isolated
gates which have lost their ramparts.

The visitor is likely to be going principally to HMS *Victory* in the Naval
Dockyard, which has a fine bustling Georgian character.

It would be good to see more of the defences exposed as shallow earthworks
and more effort made to interpret on the ground the country's principal
fortress-complex of the eighteenth century. There should be a co-ordinated
effort to recover and display as a major attraction for visitors something more of

the Portsea defences round the Dockyard—the Gosport ramparts across the harbour-mouth, the seafront forts, the main Victorian ramparts—to put Fort Brockhurst, the survivor of the outer Victorian line, in context.

Titchfield Abbey The small abbey was founded in 1232, a hundred years after the main rush into religion, for the rather severe Premonstratensians by a Bishop of Winchester, Peter des Roches. He was a French knight who became a tough supporter of King John and later an opponent of Hubert de Burgh.

Apart from some very fine tile floors and low walls there is nothing left to see. At the Dissolution the monastery and Titchfield manor were snapped up by Sir Thomas Wriothesley, a notable public figure who rose to be Earl of Southampton. His grandfather had been a Mr Writhe, whose son, a herald, settled on Wriothesley for a name and 'backdated' it on to all his ancestors.

Titchfield, like Netley Abbey (page 80), was converted into a mansion by fantastic and misplaced ingenuity. Between 1537 and 1542 the new gatehouse, a spectacular piece of work, was punched through the old nave. Only part of the cloister-buildings are accessible.

Isle of Wight

Appuldurcombe House The imposing ruins of a Queen Anne house.

Carisbrooke Castle Dominating the centre of the Isle of Wight, Carisbrooke Castle stands on the site of a late Roman fort which formed one of a chain of 'Saxon Shore Forts'. It has only lately been proved to be Roman and the detailed history is obscure. It was clearly still of great importance in early Saxon times, but later was abandoned. The Norman castle was first mentioned in the Domesday Book, AD 1086. Throughout the Middle Ages the castle was usually in the hands of a succession of great noble families, reverting to the Crown between 1078 and 1100, and 1293 and 1355. From 1405 the Lordship of the island and the castle normally rotated among members of the Royal Family. During the sixteenth century the Lordship remained in the hands of the Crown and the captains of the castle acted as governors of the island. During the Civil War the Isle of Wight was in Parliamentary hands and under the Commonwealth formed a place of imprisonment for Charles I.

The prominent motte in the centre of one of the long sides of the Roman fort seems to have been the main early Norman work; probably a timber stockade surmounted it and the ruined Roman walls. There seems to be good evidence for the building of a stone keep on the motte and a stone curtain wall

round the castle by the 1130s. About one-third of the Roman fort was provided with lesser defences as an outwork or barbican, while about two-thirds of it formed the main castle with a bank and deep ditch cut across the Roman site to separate them. The domestic buildings of the castle have unusually not been abandoned; the great hall goes back in outline to late Norman times and the other buildings contain much work of the thirteenth and fourteenth centuries, although extensively reconstructed in both Elizabethan and Victorian times. They form the museum of the Isle of Wight.

Outside and completely obscuring the Roman ditch system lies a massive line of artillery defences with five bastions, built by Federigo Gianibelli in 1597–1600.

St Catherine's Chapel, Chale The hill-top tower of a medieval lighthouse-chapel, not unlike the intact chapel and lighthouse at Abbotsbury (page 61).

Osborne House Queen Victoria's favourite villa retreat, designed by Prince Albert and built by the great speculative builder Thomas Cubitt. It is crowded with paintings and furnishings.

Yarmouth Castle A small fort or battery built for Henry VIII to cover the harbour, the Solent and the west of the island. It does not look as if it would have been much use if the need had arisen.

The visitor to Hampshire should see Basing House, Beaulieu Abbey, Mottisfont Abbey, Odiham Castle, Rockbourne Roman Villa and the noteworthy monuments at both Southampton and Winchester. At Southampton the town museum is in the medieval North Gate; God's House, a hospital of 1185, the Tudor House and the Wool House, with other fine house remains are also in local authority care. The medieval West Gate of Winchester is also a local museum and the College, St Cross Hospital and Pilgrims' Hall can be seen as well as the cathedral. On the Isle of Wight there are two Roman villas at Brading and Newport.

Several important projects are in progress on the prehistoric landscape of Hampshire. At Butser Hill, near Petersfield, an experimental Iron Age farm, the practical testing of early crops and techniques is changing our whole understanding of the period. Early strains of wheat and other crops were far more productive and nutritious than was thought. Around Danebury, near Stockbridge, careful study of the early field remains is making us realize how regular and systematic the first field layouts were.

Hertfordshire

Berkhamsted Castle The castle controls an important medieval route through the Chilterns to Northampton and the Midlands. As a major castle fairly close to London, it was always kept in minor royal hands or granted to reliable dependants, from William the Conqueror's brother, Robert of Mortain, to Thomas Becket as chancellor, Richard 'King of the Romans', and finally the Duchy of Cornwall.

The castle had very extensive stone buildings and was a grand residence, probably until 1495. Almost all this has gone and the tumbled grass ramparts are partly Norman earthworks, partly collapsed rubble. The castle park is still stocked with deer and is in National Trust care as Ashridge Park. Beneath the amazing Regency mansion is an undercroft of a small monastic college set up by Edmund, Earl of Cornwall, whom we have met at Restormel (page 48).

St Albans (Verulamium) Roman Walls The whole Roman town deserves careful study and reassessment. It is a vast open site used with splendid incongruity for recreation, with playing fields, a boating lake, a mini-zoo and so on—which rather swamps the historical importance. In state hands there is only a long stretch of the Roman town walls, but the visitor will not miss the museum, the Roman theatre and a centrally heated mosaic floor in a plain modern building among the playing fields.

The great cathedral on the other hill was once the first abbey of England, and has always been kept up, though fiercely restored. The small town that

84

grew up at the abbey gates, the Saxon church above the Roman forum, the nearby earthworks of the pre-Roman town and many other features give the whole area a very good claim to most special treatment as a prime national asset. It is almost unthinkable that we allowed a new road to be chopped across the Roman town.

Humberside

Burton Agnes Manor House   A fine Norman hall of *c.* AD 1170–80 over an aisled and vaulted lower storey. The outside is mostly cased in Jacobean brick. This type of grand house, both in town and country, was familiar to the rich throughout twelfth-century Europe.

Howden Church   The tall ruined chancel and chapter-house of a fine medieval church.

Skipsea Castle   Some of the earthworks of a large Norman motte-and-bailey castle, like Scarborough (page 169) a possession of the Lords of Holderness.

Thornton Abbey   The abbey was founded in 1139 when William, Count of Aumale, who had beaten the Scots at the Battle of the Standard the year before, sent down a dozen canons from the newly founded Kirkham Priory (page 166) close by his Yorkshire castles of Scarborough (page 169) and Skipsea.

Nothing survives of the first century's buildings within which the founder was buried. Of the complete rebuilding in the thirteenth and fourteenth centuries there are substantial ruins of the octagonal chapter-house and something of the south transept. The rest is little more than foundations excavated in the 1820s, very early days for such research.

There is nothing to see of the surrounding buildings beyond the cloister-ranges, apart from the spectacular gatehouse of the 1380s, a fine sight with its eight projecting turrets.

Kent

Horne's Place Chapel, Appledore   A delicately detailed private chapel of 1366 behind a manor-house.

Kit's Coty House and Little Kit's Coty House ('The Countless Stones'), Aylesford   The ruined and completely ruined burial chambers of two nearby long barrows.

St Augustine's Abbey and St Pancras Church, Canterbury Behind the handsome Victorian theological college, St Augustine's College, have been excavated
the extensive foundations of the great medieval abbey of St Augustine. The
ruins are not imposing except for the crypt of Abbot Scotland's church built
in early Norman times after AD 1070. In the centre of these medieval foundations the visitor can pick out with difficulty the much earlier remains of several
churches of the Anglo-Saxon abbey founded in AD 598 for St Augustine himself. Under the centre of the nave of the later church lie the fragmentary
walls of the main church of SS Peter and Paul, where the early Archbishops
of Canterbury and Kings of Kent were buried. To the east, under the later
medieval tower, only the west wall of the church of St Mary exists. To the
east again, beyond the medieval Lady Chapel there are substantial ruins
of the Anglo-Saxon church of St Pancras. These three early churches are
in a line.

This kind of group or 'family' of churches is normal in early monasteries
in England and Europe. Later, all the churches and chapels were more often
combined in a single building. An early attempt to combine the churches of
SS Peter and Paul and St Mary forms the most substantial part of the Anglo-
Saxon foundations, a great rotunda built to link them by Abbot Wolfric in
about 1050. This was never finished, but seems to have been intended as a great
galleried building on the lines of another at Dijon, which also linked two earlier
churches. Within little more than a generation it and the early churches on both
sides were completely demolished and even their foundations partly destroyed
for the massive early Norman church.

Beneath the medieval cloister-buildings which can be picked out in outline a number of Saxon monastic buildings have been partly excavated. They are covered up, but their position can be identified on the plan exhibited on the site.

Deal Castle and Walmer Castle Henry VIII's ambitious scheme for the defence of south-east England included a defence line dominating the anchorage sheltered by the Goodwin Sands known as the Downs. Three stone forts were built and linked by a rampart with four earthwork batteries. Sandown Castle, the northern fort, has been largely destroyed by the sea, but could be more carefully displayed; Walmer Castle, the southern fort, is intact, with many later additions and still serves as a residence. Deal Castle, the central strong-point, is a fine complete example of the defences of 1539–40. The plan of a large central drum tower with six attached drum turrets is surrounded by an outer curtain made up of six large round bastions, all of them lavishly pierced for guns. The unusual design of Henry's castles was put to the test only in the amateurish conditions of the Civil War. A similar group of three forts was also built at the same time at Hull.

The museum in the gatehouse of Deal Castle contains a good series of finds from the district. It is interesting to note the wide trading connections of the lost medieval port of Stonar, which disappeared after the floods of 1359, 1365 and 1366 and the sack by the French in 1385. The little town of Deal grew up to the north of the castle by 1700, and Middle Street is our most complete street of artisan housing of the seventeenth century. (Fig. 5.)

Walmer Castle has many relics of various Lords Warden of the Cinque Ports, notably the Duke of Wellington, who died here. Here too are the most gorgeous romantic nineteenth-century grounds, enhanced by the wheeling seagulls.

Dover Castle Dover Castle is the grim cold first sight of England for so many visitors: more of our regular comings and goings to the rest of the world have passed through Dover than any other port, over the last couple of thousand years. It is the only castle in the country to have remained primarily in mili-tary occupation by the state from the time of William the Conqueror to Eliza-beth II, although Windsor Castle and the Tower of London have been continu-ously in government hands for as long.

At Dover the castle and the town are inextricably interlocked, and at different times first one and then the other has been pre-eminent. It is a duality that is very common across Europe: at Athens, Rome, Salzburg and Prague, to name a few, there is an Acropolis or a Capitol above and a town or towns below. There was probably a large hill-fort at Dover in the Iron Age although very little trace of this has turned up. In Roman times the great lighthouse was built on a high point, but the main forts were down below beside the old harbour,

where spectacular remains have recently been excavated. Some of it has been buried again beneath a new road, and we hope that as much as possible of the rest will be saved.

Saxon occupation was found across the Roman forts below and in about the early eleventh century the fine cruciform church was built above, beside the lighthouse. Was the hill-fort in use as a refuge? Is the church a refuge or alternative for St Martin's down below? Was the whole town moved up here at some time? We need to know more.

The first Norman castle is no better known. All we can say is that Odo, the Conqueror's half-brother and Bishop of Bayeux, imposed the duty of castle-guard at Dover on the tenants of his huge estates as far away as Hampshire and Lincolnshire and very widely in Essex, Sussex and Kent.

Henry II, with Edward I perhaps the greatest of our castle-builders, created the castle we see today. His first stage seems to have been the north-east part of the outer walls, where a stretch of about 500 feet (140 metres) is thought to be of AD 1168–80. What were the rest of the defences at this time? In c. 1180–90 the keep and inner walls were built, but massive earthmoving had to be done first, digging out the great inner ditch. Was the spoil levelled up around the keep, or down, against the outer wall-line? The inner walls have powerful gates well protected by outworks and shallow square open-backed towers very similar to Framlingham Castle of 1190 (page 139). All this cost about £7,000, which can be compared with £1,400 for the new castle at Orford (page

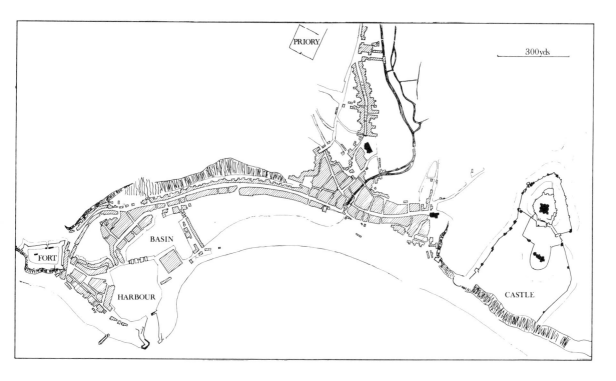

11 Dover: the castle,
town and harbours
from a plan of 1737

141) in 1166–73. The shallow square towers of the inner and outer walls and
the projecting turrets of the keep gave a triple tier of covering fire. This was
an early use of projecting towers, but only for this period and country. The
engineer Maurice, who built the keep, had seen many late Roman bastions,
solid at Pevensey (page 142) or hollow at Portchester (page 80). The tiers of
concentric defences at Dover were a great innovation in the west, modelled
perhaps on the walls of Constantinople, of the fifth century AD.

King John lost Normandy, and had to see to Dover. In 1208–15 he spent
£1,000 or more and this seems to have finished the north-west length of the
outer wall. Dover was besieged in 1216–17 by the French prince whose miners
brought down the brand new North Gate. Hubert de Burgh, the Justiciar, bar-
ricaded the ruins and his knights held the gate. After the siege he repaired
the outer wall, spending perhaps £1,500 in 1217–21, while the work in 1221–
5 cost £1,300 and in 1226–56, £4,700. All this gave Dover two lesser gates
with underground passages for sudden counter-attacks and the immensely
powerful main entrance, the Constable's Gate, as well as the full ring of outer
walls to the sea. De Burgh's work can be studied at Hadleigh (page 72) and
in Gwent.

Dover has been steadily repaired, suffering most neglect in the early eighteenth century. As late as 1800 the castle mounted 230 guns and was reckoned

89

to be good for fourteen days holding-out. A fortress was built on the Western Heights as part of the Martello tower chain, and even in the 1860s great new outer works were constructed. Only in 1958 did the army start handing their most ancient fortress over, to become a monument.

Dymchurch Martello Tower   One of the long chain of south coast strongpoints put up in 1805–10. They were planned at a great crisis when Napoleon was mustering his armies at Boulogne, and actually built when there was no chance at all that the French could land.

Ebbsfleet Cross   A modern memorial of St Augustine's landing in AD 597. We have been told ever since that he brought Christianity to the English, but how true is this?

Eynsford Castle   A very trim and friendly baby castle of a knightly family, tenants of the Archbishops of Canterbury. William de Eynsford III played a significant part on both sides in the quarrel between Henry II and Thomas Becket. William de Eynsford V sided with the French prince against King John and was duly captured by him at Rochester (page 93). Eynsford, like Totnes (page 61), was inherited by the de la Zouches in the fourteenth century.

We see a low broad mound, walled round, and a much ruined house in the centre, all of Norman date. In fact the castle had an outer bailey, which is not accessible, and now contains an interesting half-timbered house of *c.* 1500. Were there only stables here before, or was there another residential block? Excavations at the drawbridge have produced well-preserved timbers of a series of early bridges which have led to a most important study. (Fig. 6.)

Lullingstone Roman Villa   The Roman farmstead was very completely excavated in 1949–60 and tells a story of the greatest interest in the economy and social life of the Empire.

There was a small farm here before or early on in the Roman occupation. This prospered, was rebuilt in stone in *c.* AD 80, and a round temple was built nearby. The place was briefly occupied in 180–200 by a high-ranking Roman and lavishly rebuilt. Many a farm within reach of London was reconstructed in this way in medieval times and in every later century, and it is constantly happening today. At Lullingstone, kitchens, baths and chapel-rooms were added. A basement-store was converted into a shrine to the water-nymphs. Two magnificent portrait busts in Greek marble strongly hint that the new owner came from Italy or Greece.

The house then lay derelict for some time but was reconstructed, perhaps in about 280, as a prosperous farming establishment. A large grain-store was built close by and soon after, up on the hill nearby, a solid tomb-temple was built as a kind of family shrine. In *c*. 330–60 the centre of the house was reconstructed to give two reception rooms with fine mosaic floors. In the semi-circular dining-room is Jupiter as a Bull making off with a very willing Europa; the reception room has the demigod Bellerophon on Pegasus, his winged horse, killing a legendary monster. Dolphins and Seasons complete the pattern. In *c*. 370 a Christian chapel was fitted up in the villa, which may have been abandoned and burnt down by *c*. 400–20.

The excavator skilfully interpreted the life of the villa from the finds, and many of them are displayed in the modern building that covers the villa, but sadly cuts it off from its setting. The marble busts and the wall-paintings of the Christian chapel are now in the British Museum.

Maison Dieu, Ospringe   Some of the buildings of the small Royal Hospital stand precariously beside the Roman Watling Street (now the A2), in the hamlet of Ospringe on the outskirts of Faversham. The main buildings of the hospital seem to have been on the north side of the road. On the south side the visitor can see a complete timber-framed house of *c*. 1516, when the hospital was dissolved, standing over a medieval undercroft.

The showcases contain a display of finds from the Roman town or posting station, half a mile to the west. On the other side of the Roman settlement the visitor should notice the ruined early Saxon church which incorporates a Roman mausoleum.

Old Soar Manor, Plaxtol   The residential end of a manor-house of the thirteenth century. A Georgian farmhouse has replaced the hall. (National Trust.)

Reculver Roman Fort and Anglo-Saxon Church   The fort was built early in the third century AD, but it is not impressive: the walls are reduced to a low crumbled core and the ditches are filled. It commanded the northern end of the Wensum channel 'three furlongs broad', which separated Thanet from the mainland of Kent.

The remains of a broad apsidal Saxon church with side chambers are carefully laid out. The church was wantonly pulled down in 1805, and what makes Reculver memorable are the twin late Norman towers built grandly on to the west end of the church. These were kept as a landmark for sailors, and repaired by Trinity House. The coastline they look down on has changed, for the sea has eroded into the low clay cliffs and washed down almost half the Roman fort. The Wensum channel, where the southward drift of the east coast meets the eastward drift of the south coast, was completely silted up and reclaimed as fields between the fifteenth and seventeenth centuries.

Most of the Roman forts on the south and east coasts have both a Saxon church and a Norman castle. Why is there no castle here? Reculver has given

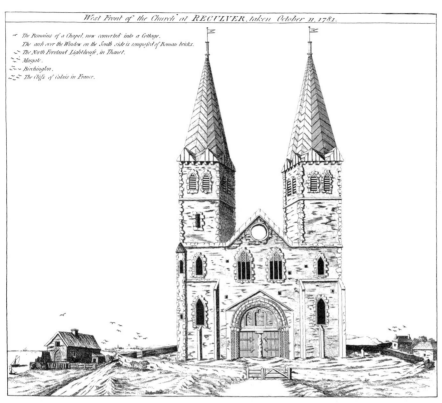

West front of the church at Reculver, taken October 11, 1781.

West front of the
church at Reculver,
Kent: an engraving of
1781

Reculver Church,
Kent

an emblem to the Kent Archaeology Rescue Team, whose C.II.B badges indicate the Second Cohort of Batavians, who were stationed here.

The site is swamped in a sea of caravans, a dismal setting which should be reconsidered.

Richborough Roman Fort and Town On a low island or near-island inside the southern end of the former Wensum channel between Kent and the Isle of Thanet are the remains of a key site for the Roman and Anglo-Saxon periods. We can see parts of three Roman forts, a huge triumphal arch, a Roman town and, as usual in these forts, an Anglo-Saxon church. It is not easy to disentangle all this, and it is all too easy to forget that the whole hill-top, not just the official site, is the Roman town.

This must have been the main invasion base when the Romans came in AD 43, and a pair of ditches have been dug out, part of a huge enclosure of this date. A generation later an immense triumphal arch was built, as a landmark and to celebrate the conquest. This has gone, apart from the foundations, which mark out in reverse where the mighty legs of the arch stood. Only a few fragments of marble and small bits of statues have been dug up. Round the arch were built some stone houses of the town and two of these have been left as foundations to see. The houses were cleared away and a small triple-ditched fort built round the arch in *c.* 220–30. Later, perhaps in *c.* 280–90, a larger stone fort was built, and its high bastioned walls are what we remember. This fort is often attributed to the rebel emperor Carausius by over-romantic scholars who forget that most defence schemes are built when the need for them is past.

Richborough was gradually silted up; its functions as a port transferred to Sandwich and as an administrative centre perhaps to Eastry (which means 'east region'). Sandwich and its twin port of Stonar silted up in turn and Deal became the roadstead-town where the larger sailing ships of the seventeenth to nineteenth centuries could lie safely in the Downs without a harbour. Richborough with its ruins, Sandwich with its sleepy medieval houses and Deal are all, in their different fabrics, the same place.

Rochester Castle The first Norman castle at Rochester may have been an enclosure made outside the Roman walls in *c.* AD 1066–7, later replaced, perhaps in 1087–9, by a fortress within the walls. The large keep in a corner of this second enclosure may date from *c.* 1127–35, and was held for the King by the Archbishops of Canterbury, which cannot have pleased the Bishops of Rochester. In 1215 King John trapped a group of rebel barons in the castle and mined down a corner of the keep to get them. It cost £530 to mend.

In 1367–93 Rochester was overhauled, the keep repaired, some towers

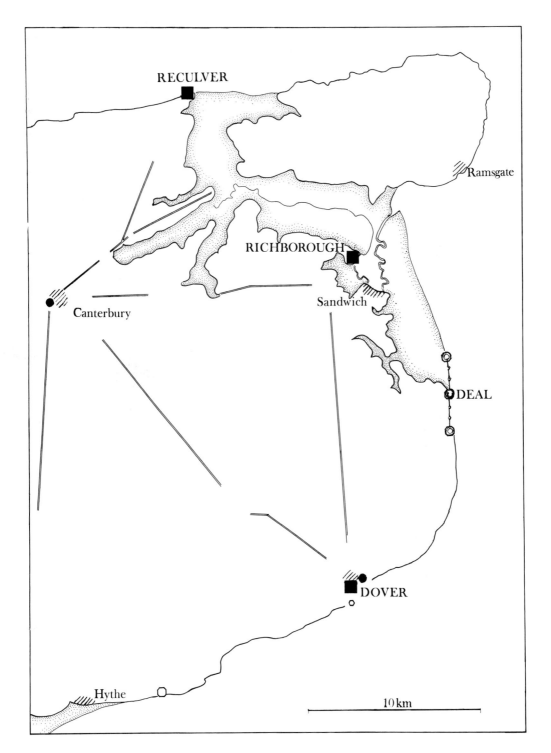

RECULVER

Ramsgate

RICHBOROUGH

Canterbury

Sandwich

DEAL

DOVER

Hythe

10 km

2 Coastal defences f east Kent with Roman roads and the Vensum channel, pen in Roman times, hown stippled. Roman forts are hown as black quares, medieval astles as black circles nd later forts as open ctagons

constructed and the bridge across the Medway built with a great drawbridge-tower, at a cost of at least £3,000. From the fifteenth to the nineteenth centuries the castle was neglected.

Some fragments of the wall surround the public park. The marvellous roofless keep is whitened by the screaming gulls.

Temple Manor, Strood   This royal manor was given to the Knights Templar in *c.* 1158 by Henry II, taken into royal hands again in 1308 and given in 1342–6 to the nuns of Denny Abbey (page 39). A block of *c.* 1240 with two fine stone chambers over a vaulted undercroft may have been a lodging for Templar dignitaries. We must imagine it surrounded by a working home farm, bailiff's house, courthouse and so on, rather than the present factories.

Upnor Castle   An unusual Elizabethan fortlet, built in 1559–67 to protect the fleet in 'mothballs' moored in the Medway below Rochester. It was walled on the landward side in 1599–1601. In 1667 the Dutch raided the Medway in force, burnt the ships laid up there and sailed off with the Royal George. This humiliating defeat showed that these coastal batteries were more use as a deterrent than in action. More and bigger forts were built further down the Medway in the seventeenth, eighteenth and nineteenth centuries. Upnor's 'fairy castle' skyline from the river is due to later seventeenth-century alterations.

pnor Castle, Kent

West Malling Tower   A solid little tower keep of *c*. AD 1100. Where is the rest of the castle?

Lancashire

Salley   Remains of a small abbey in the Ribble valley.

Warton   The shell of a small medieval house.

Whalley   A medieval abbey gatehouse.

Leicestershire

Ashby de la Zouche Castle   After the previous owner was captured during a battle in the Wars of the Roses, and beheaded, Lord Hastings, on the winning side, was granted the large manor-house and estate of Ashby de la Zouche beside the prosperous market-town. Hastings built a fine chapel on to the manor-house, and proceeded to turn it into a castle fit for his status as Edward IV's Lord Chamberlain. At his old family home Kirby Muxloe, 12 miles (19 km.) away, Hastings did just the same and there we can easily trace his defences of the 1470s, though there are only a few foundations of the older manor-house. At Ashby the manor-house stands roofless, but most of the defences have disappeared completely, blown up by Parliament after a year-long siege in the Civil War.

The Hastings Tower on the south side rises to a height of about 90 feet (30 metres), and used to comprise a complete self-contained residence. The kitchen on the west side was heightened to form another great tower. There were probably massive towers, one a gatehouse towards the church on the north and another on the east, which have gone, but the south-east corner of the walls still stands. The older manor-house forms a tremendous jigsaw puzzle with fragments of all periods, from long before, and after, Lord Hastings' time. The hall seems to date from the twelfth century, reconstructed in the fourteenth and sixteenth centuries, with windows of the seventeenth century, and the buttery, pantry and solar show very much the same history.

Kirby Muxloe Castle　A great brick castle with a wide moat was designed in 1480 to envelop the old family manor-house of the Hastings. William Hastings had risen to vast wealth and power in the Wars of the Roses, and had become a great local magnate with castles at Bagworth, 5 miles (8 km.) north-west, and Ashby de la Zouche (page 96), 7 miles (11 km.) beyond that. Ashby was Lord Hastings' favourite residence when he was not at court or away on embassies to other countries. The present castle at Kirby Muxloe, well placed for hunting in Charnwood Forest, was meant for ostentatious display rather than for defence, and was never finished. In 1483, at the height of his success, Lord Hastings was suddenly denounced, taken outside and beheaded during a Privy Council meeting which he was attending.

The foundations, the lower part of the gatehouse, one corner tower and the moat lie in a threatened oasis of peace among the booming suburbs of Leicester, close to the M1. On the left of the path down from the road, the manor-farm is still working; on the right, a field with terraces and bumps must be the site of the stables and outer court, and perhaps a formal garden. (Fig. 5.)

Jewry Wall, Leicester　A huge Roman wall with arches once, apparently, the main side wall of the basilica, or 'town hall' on to the forum. It was built in *c*. AD 130, but soon afterwards incorporated into a public baths, built very oddly across the forum. On one side is a glossy archaeological museum; tight against the other a fascinating Saxon church.

At York it now seems that the Anglo-Saxons always used the basilica as their cathedral, and the same may have been the case in London before St Pauls was built, to follow later tradition and the medieval bishops' special jurisdiction in the basilica area. At Leicester we may be looking at the side both of a Roman basilica and of a Saxon Cathedral.

Lyddington Bedehouse　A late medieval manor-house of the Bishops of Lincoln, later turned into an almshouse.

97

Lincolnshire

Bolingbroke Castle The low walls of the castle were rebuilt on a new site in *c.* AD 1230 by the Earl of Chester who built Beeston Castle (page 39), as much against the rest of England as the Welsh. Bolingbroke Castle, the centre of a great estate, has been a Lancaster possession since 1311, that is, effectively royal since Henry IV, who was born here, became king in 1399. Bolingbroke played an interesting role under siege in 1643.

The same kind of layout is found at the contemporary Hadleigh Castle (page 72).

Bishop's Palace, Lincoln A fine complex of medieval ruins across the defences of the Roman fort and upper town from the cathedral and close.

London

The royal palaces and great houses of London are still, as in the Middle Ages, the interlocking responsibility of many different state departments—the Lord Chamberlain for actual royal residences, the Bailiff of the Royal Parks, the army, the navy, the Victoria and Albert Museum and many more have a finger in the pie. We were quite unable to discover, for instance, who is responsible for Queen Mary's Steps, a charming small piece of history on the embankment. Surprisingly little research has been done on the early monuments: the Tower of London is virtually unstudied and in the Palace of Westminster it is tragic that infilling in the inner courts has not been given adequate archaeological priority, and that the car-park in New Palace Yard was dug out with very little observation. We need to learn a great deal more about how these primary monuments of our civilization came to be formed. It will teach us more about ourselves.

We have listed these London monuments as simply as possible. A number more early royal houses, at Chelsea, Somerset House and Leicester Square, are virtually unknown. Nonsuch and Richmond are more widely known.

Apsley House A grand brick house of 1771–8. The Duke of Wellington bought it in 1817 and in 1828–9 extended and faced it with stone. (Wellington Museum, Victoria and Albert Museum.)

Chelsea Hospital Built for army veterans—its present use—in 1682–91 by Sir Christopher Wren. There was a scheme while it was under construction to make it the basis of a great citadel for James II.

Chiswick House
London

98

Chiswick House Lord Burlington's grand garden villa of *c.* 1725 was originally built as an annexe to a large older house. A fragment of the garden layout survives.

Eltham Palace A royal palace of the fourteenth century with a fine great hall of the 1470s. Excavation has begun to reveal the ranges of other rooms.

Greenwich Palace and Park To be near Eltham, Humphrey, Duke of Gloucester, Henry V's brother, acquired a country house here and enclosed a park. From 1447 to 1642 this was a favourite royal residence. In 1616–19 James I's queen, Anne of Denmark, got Inigo Jones to start the present Queen's House, one of the first truly classical buildings in England, as a garden pavilion to span the main road and link palace and park. This was completed in 1629–37.

Charles II started to rebuild the palace for himself in 1664–9, but William and Mary preferred Hampton Court and Greenwich was completed as a Naval Hospital in 1698–1814. The park has much of its 1660s layout and Wren's Observatory of 1675–6.

Ham House A great mansion of *c.* 1610 was much rebuilt inside in 1637–8 and doubled up in 1673–5 by the Duke of Lauderdale whose fittings and

furniture make it a rare treasure house. (National Trust and Victoria and Albert Museum.) The garden is being put back to its seventeenth-century state.

Hampton Court and Parks Cardinal Wolsey bought the manor from the Knights of St John and built the grandest palace in northern Europe. This led to his downfall and Hampton Court was a favourite royal residence from 1529 to 1760. Henry VIII's great hall, side wings, cellars, kitchens and tennis courts of 1529–36 are linked to William and Mary's high Fountain Court of 1689–1702. Wolsey's huge parks, now Home Park and Bushy Park, have something of the fine layout of the 1660s.

Hyde Park and Kensington Palace The park was enclosed from well-drained arable land by Henry VIII in 1536, part of his high-handed transformation of the landscape west of London. Where are the Tudor hunting-lodges? The palace was a small country house beyond the end of the park, bought by William III in 1689. The vast additions Wren built for him in 1690–5 must, as so often with monarchs, have ruined the peace he sought. More was rebuilt in 1718–26. In 1729 Kensington Gardens was cut out of Hyde Park and Bridgeman's layout with criss-cross avenues can still be seen.

Kew Palace and Gardens The old park of Richmond Palace was redesigned by Bridgeman for the future Queen Caroline in 1722, but this was swept away in the 1770s by 'Capability' Brown. The grounds of another minor royal house, landscaped in the 1760s by Sir William Chambers with temples, pavilions, an orangery and the great pagoda, were thrown into it in the 1770s. No less than

Hampton Court, London

three Georgian royal houses were rather casually demolished and all that is left is a modest country house built at the end of the old park in 1631 by a London merchant. This had served as an overflow for the other royal houses for some time but was a 'palace' for sixteen years as George III came there in 1802–18. It contains many touching personal mementoes of the Georges.

Kew Gardens have been established since 1841.

Lancaster House   A great town-house of 1817–30 built by Benjamin Wyatt for the Duke of York, it was finished by Smirke for the Dukes of Sutherland who lived here until 1912.

Marlborough House   Queen Anne gave a strip of St James's Park to her favourite, the Duchess of Marlborough, who had Wren build the house with two storeys in 1709–11. The Dukes of Marlborough kept this as their town-house until 1817, rebuilding the attics as a full storey in 1770. Between 1860 and 1880 the house was pulled about and heightened again for the Prince of Wales.

Osterley House   An Elizabethan country house which was largely rebuilt in the 1720s but transformed for Robert Child in 1763–77 by Robert Adam with its astonishing portico and lavishly decorated rooms which have kept the furniture he designed for them. The park deserves study. (National Trust, Victoria and Albert Museum.)

Regent's Park   Henry VIII created Marylebone Park in 1538, enclosing pasture and woodland of several properties within a circular park bank. Can we discover his hunting-lodges and banqueting house? John Nash developed the property for the Prince Regent in 1812–26, still leaving a large park, which he laid out.

Richmond Park   With a choice of residence at the Tudor palaces of Richmond and Hampton Court, Charles I recklessly enclosed a new park in 1635–7, taking in heath, woodland and arable fields.

St James's Park and Buckingham Palace   The earliest of Henry VIII's London parks was enclosed from meadowland and low-lying arable in 1531. The old hospital of St James was rebuilt as an extra palace, perhaps for entertainments. The formal layout of 1660–2 remains in the Mall, but the straight canal was curved into the present lake by Nash in 1828 when he had finished Regent's Park and built the shell of Buckingham Palace. This had been a private house until it was bought as a Queen's house in 1762, so that the old Somerset House

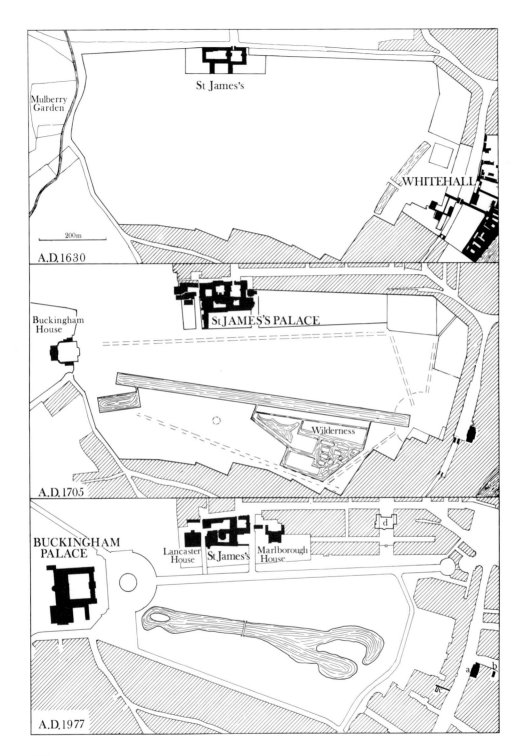

St James's

Mulberry
Garden

200m

A.D.1630

WHITEHALL

Buckingham
House

St JAMES'S PALACE

Wilderness

A.D.1705

BUCKINGHAM
PALACE

Lancaster
House

St James's

Marlborough
House

d

a   b
c

A.D.1977

102

could be developed as offices. Does anything survive of the Duke of Buckingham's house of 1705, of Lord Arlington's house of 1674, or of Lord Goring's house of 1630? All these lie beneath the well-known façade of 1913.

Tower of London   William the Conqueror built three strongpoints around the Roman walls when the Londoners submitted to him. Baynards Castle and Montfitchet Castle have gone, but the third remains, with the Crown Jewels a symbol of royal authority still. The Tower of London has seldom overawed the citizens as much as it was meant to. Within a small earthwork was built the tower itself in *c.* 1077–97, the great palace-castle that we call the White Tower. At Colchester is the bottom of an even larger keep, at Chepstow (page 194) another.

It is far from clear what went on here in the twelfth century. In *c.* 1220–30 Henry III built an inner bailey south of the White Tower, with residential ranges. In 1238–41 £5,000 was spent, in 1262 £1,000, and this must account for the main inner line of the walls. In 1275–85 Edward I dug a great new moat and built the low outer walls, encroaching into the city and into the river where a new dock-gate, the Traitor's Gate, reminds us of the sea-linked castles of North Wales (pages 202–10). All this work cost a recorded £21,000, giving the defences their present shape, although there have been many lesser changes since. The Tower would repay continuing programmes of research and survey.

The Zoo, the Mint, the Public Record Office and the Ordnance Survey have all come out of the Tower. The Ravens and the Armouries (Museum) remain.

Westminster Palace How can we learn more about the early days of Westminster? So little is known that it seems safe to doubt whether it was ever a separate 'island' in the marshes as tradition says. Does the church which gives the place its name date back to the seventh, or only to the tenth century AD? Edward the Confessor rebuilt the church as a royal abbey, and seems to have had a palace here, but where was it?

William II built Westminster Hall before 1098, a vast and impressive sight today. Beside it Edward I started to rebuild St Stephen's chapel in 1292, which was finished by Edward III in 1348. The lower chapel, which is still intact, seems to have been vaulted in *c.* 1320. St Stephen's cloister dates from *c.* 1395, and the hall roof and windows from 1394–1401. The boundaries of the palace are not very clearly known except in the south-west corner, where the Jewel Tower of 1365–6 is preserved and accessible. A good deal of gold, silver and precious stones was housed here with the Privy Wardrobe until it was sold off in 1551. The top floor is the strongroom, the middle floor offices and the Keeper of the Wardrobe lodged on the ground floor. The abbey chapter-house was built in *c.* 1245–55 by Henry III and has always been as much a public as an abbey building. The sculpture, wall-paintings and tiled floor are notable.

Whitehall On Cardinal Wolsey's fall in 1529, Henry VIII took over and moved into the town-house of the Archbishop of York, which Wolsey had rebuilt and vastly extended. This was the main London palace of the Tudors and Stuarts. Of Wolsey's work a fine vaulted cellar remains beneath the Ministry of Defence and can be seen by arrangement. The rest of the palace was burnt out in 1698 and gradually replaced by grand Georgian town-houses, which have mostly gone for Victorian and modern ministries.

Henry VIII's vast extensions included great passages, as at the Queen's House at Greenwich a century later, to link the palace with the park across the main road. To make St James's Park in 1531, as we have seen, fields were bought up and roads closed. On the park side Henry VIII, a keen sportsman, built a gigantic 'fun-palace' with tennis courts, cockpits and so on. This is now under the Treasury, aptly enough, and from Downing Street a Tudor passage-way and tennis court can be seen.

Within this rambling Tudor palace, and in complete contrast to it, Inigo Jones built the Banqueting House for James I in 1619–22, for shows and feasts. This grandly classical building was something completely new. Rubens' ceiling paintings were commissioned specially for it in 1629 and sent over in 1635.

On the river front in the 1690s Queen Mary reclaimed a garden from the mud flats, and the water-steps at one end can be seen in Whitehall Place.

Jewel Tower, Westminster Palace, London
(*top*) Jewel Tower on left
(*bottom*) same viewpoint during excavations in 1962

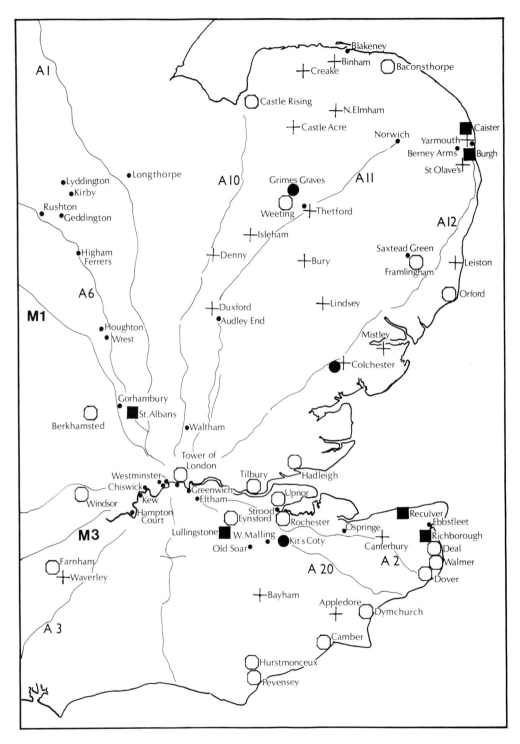

14 Map of the south-east of England. (See key on Map 1 for types of monument)

Norfolk

Baconsthorpe Castle John Heydon, an astute and much hated survivor through the Wars of the Roses, lapped his minor manor of Wood Hall round with castle-defences in *c.* 1450–60, just as Lord Hastings did at Ashby de la Zouche (page 96) and Kirby Muxloe (page 97). His gate-tower and part of the wide moat and walls survive.

A second outer gatehouse was built as part of an extensive forecourt and garden layout by his great-grandson about a hundred years later. A century later again *his* great-grandson in turn had to pull most of the 'castle' down to help pay his losses under the Commonwealth, as he had been Charles I's Lieutenant General of Ordnance. He must have learnt something about the value of family castles in the Civil War. (Fig. 6.)

Berney Arms Windmill, Reedham A fine brick windmill, long used for drainage, but this was not its original function.

Berney Arms
Windmill, Norfolk

Binham Priory and Cross   This cell or outpost of the great Benedictine abbey of St Albans was founded in *c*. AD 1100 by a kinsman of William the Conqueror. It was spaciously planned and the parish still uses the middle part of the nave. The ruins around have been cleared and laid out neatly.

Blakeney Guildhall   The brick-built undercroft of the fourteenth century remains.

Caister-by-Yarmouth   Some house foundations and a gate of the Roman town.

Castle Acre Priory and Castle Gate   William de Warenne, the younger son of a minor Norman knight, rose to a position of special trust with William the Conqueror before 1066 and was one of the eleven men among whom a quarter of England was divided up in the greatest baronies, especially on the northern

Castle Acre Priory, Norfolk

frontier and on the south coast. The de Warennes, turbulently but often loyally, held their place in both these 'sensitive' areas with Conisbrough in Yorkshire and Lewes in Sussex. At Lewes they founded one of the first of the great Norman monasteries in 1078–80. In *c*. 1090 the first or the second William de Warenne founded another Cluniac priory at Castle Acre, and Scolland, steward of Richmond (page 169), was an early benefactor.

The remains are a very complete Norman monastic layout. Cluny drained off much of the funds and those high-handed castle-builders Edwards I, II and III persecuted all 'alien' houses, to pay for their extravaganzas. These factors left the priory very little money for rebuilding their very solid early buildings of *c*. 1090–1140. The west front and the transepts of the church stand quite high. The dormitory and latrines are very impressive, but the dining-hall is not so well preserved. That accounts for the east and south cloister-buildings. The west range, the prior's lodging, is of great interest, with many alterations throughout the Middle Ages. The later additions to the block are complete and roofed.

One of the de Warenne's castle-gates is in state hands. The village has encroached within the castle earthworks. (Fig. 2.)

Castle Rising An excellent castle with a tremendous rampart around a fine keep. The village was once a prosperous harbour town.

Creake Abbey An Augustinian priory from AD 1227, Creake was raised to the status of an abbey in 1231. It developed rather accidentally out of a chapel built here in *c*. 1206 which was the nucleus of a hospital established in *c*. 1217.

Two notable ladies deserve mention: Lady Alice de Nerford, the foundress of the place in all four stages, is said to have intended the hospital to celebrate a naval victory at Sandwich by her nephew, Hubert de Burgh, a great builder at Dover (page 87), Hadleigh (page 72) and in Gwent (page 192). Lady Margaret Beaufort, Henry VII's mother, founder in her turn of two Cambridge colleges, took over the abbey property for Christ's College a generation before the dissolution, when the canons died out in 1506.

Parts of the chancel and transepts stand to a good height and it is interesting to see the early chapel, which is the chancel, vastly extended for the abbey. It was all burnt down in 1484 and only a section was patched up for the last twenty years.

Greyfriars, Great Yarmouth The west cloister walk can still be seen.

Small Houses, Great Yarmouth In the narrow alleys, once typical of the town, a few early seventeenth-century houses have been studied and preserved. Row

117, 8 and 9 display some rescued fittings. Row 111, 6, 7 and 8 are also in state care. 4 South Quay is a museum (National Trust).

Grime's Graves, Weeting One out of hundreds of shafts dug into the chalk here in Neolithic times can be inspected. The flint mined from the shafts was processed, much of it on the spot, into tools, and was one of many sources of raw material for the characteristic heavy polished axe of the period, used mainly, perhaps, for clearing woodland for cultivation. The British Museum, which has many of the older finds, is carrying out an important research project here.

North Elmham Saxon Cathedral The low walls remain of a church, which seems to be the late Saxon cathedral abandoned first for Thetford and then in the 1090s, for Norwich. The walls probably date from *c.* AD 1020–50; earlier floor levels found beneath may go back to the early tenth century, but excavations revealed no obvious traces of a major early church. The cathedral had only a very shallow apse, no structural chancel and, with its wide transept, distantly copies Old St Peter's in Rome.

110

Cow Tower, Norwich A brick tower of *c.* 1400 on the river bank, which once formed part of the town defences. Much more of the walls can be followed.

Thetford Priory Roger Bigod of Framlingham (page 139) founded a Cluniac priory in *c.* AD 1103 and built on this site in 1107–14 to match Castle Acre (page 108). The gatehouse is complete, the church and cloister-buildings are low but extensively cleared; it is set in a sea of bungalows.

Thetford Warren Lodge A small medieval hunting-tower built on open heath-land, but now set among pinewoods.

Weeting Castle A few ruins of a moated house remain. The family were tenants of the Warennes of Castle Acre (page 108).

Northamptonshire

Eleanor Cross, Geddington That perpetual showman Edward I put up a string of crosses on the course of his Queen Eleanor of Castile's funeral procession. Another is at Hardingstone. They show a wonderful geometrical ingenuity, playing triangles and hexagons.

The royal hunting-lodge here is marked by bumpy pasture north-east of the fine church, which has important Saxon work. The village is perfect: how many village schools teach maypole-dancing to the tune of 'Sellinger's Round'? The great house of Boughton is now open.

Chichele College, Higham Ferrers The remains of a college of 1422, established by the founder of All Souls College, Oxford, can be seen here.

Kirby Hall A fine half-ruined mansion of 1570–1640 with a skeletal garden layout of 1686. What will it be like when all the hills around have been scalped by ironstone mining?

Rushton Triangular Lodge Sir Thomas Tresham, a Catholic and grandson of the last Prior of the Knights of St John, worked out his religious enthusiasm in some amazing buildings. Lyveden New Bield (National Trust) symbolizes the Passion; this Warrener's Lodge represents the Trinity with the most involved Latin allusions, with three sides, each with three gables. Tourists have been carving their initials on it since 1675. The setting is incongruous, with alien Scots pines and monkey-puzzle trees. It would be good to know more about the whole estate, not least Tresham's garden at Lyveden.

111

Northumberland

Berwick on Tweed The wonderfully preserved Elizabethan defences show many changes of plan during construction, which is to be expected on a military project. Earlier ramparts and walls are preserved in some lengths, notably the long castle wall dropping steeply to the Tweed. (Fig. 4.)

Brinkburn Priory A priory of Augustinian canons was founded in AD 1135 in the romantic valley of the Coquet river. The first buildings of the monastery have left no trace and what we see is a rebuilding of *c.* 1200. Unlike most monastic sites, the church is complete and roofed; it too was ruined until it was rebuilt in 1858. On the site of the cloisters stands a large part-Gothick Regency mansion.

Dunstanburgh Castle This vast lonely stronghold was built by Edward II's uncle, Thomas, Earl of Lancaster, in 1313–16, by walling off a dramatic projecting cliff of the Northumberland coast. There was an earlier hill-fort here, to judge from the name, but this may have been levelled by cultivation; much ridge-and-furrow from ploughing the open fields of Embleton can be seen in the turf outside and inside the defences. In *c.* 1380 another great half-royal magnate, John of Gaunt, walled up the gatehouse and built it into a tiny citadel or inner ward with a new gateway alongside. Dunstanburgh was besieged by the Scots, and fell to both Yorkists and Lancastrians in the Wars of the Roses, just as a good castle should. It was always rather a liability—on no route, without a decent harbour and very remote—and was abandoned, probably with some relief, after 1470.

Castle and Royal
Border Bridge,
Berwick on Tweed

The visitor has a long and very stimulating coastal walk from either north (three-quarters of a mile) or south (about a mile). (National Trust.)

Holy Island of Lindisfarne　On this distant windswept island some of the greatest works of European art were created by the monks established here by St Aidan. The Lindisfarne Gospels are in the British Museum, and the treasures of St Cuthbert, Bishop here between AD 685 and 687, are at Durham. The monks fled as long ago as 875 to escape Viking raiders from the sea, but held together and finally settled in 995 at the marvellous hill-top fortress of Durham under their twenty-fourth bishop.

The monks of Durham continued to own Lindisfarne and Islandshire on the mainland, and built one of their daughter priories here. There are now two churches and the ancient monastery probably always had a number of churches and chapels on its site between the village and a high rock called the Hough.

The parish church dates from the twelfth, thirteenth and fourteenth centuries: close by, the priory church of the twelfth century is in ruins, with both ends and parts of the centre standing to a good height. A good deal can be

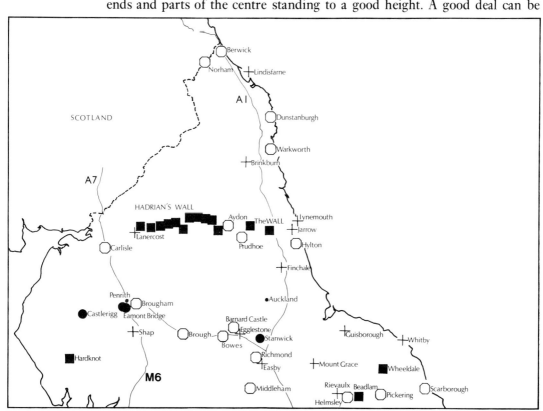

15　Map of the far north of England. (See key on Map 1 for types of monument)

115

made out from the foundations of the cloister-buildings and outer court, built in the thirteenth century, and fortified in the fourteenth against raids from the Scots.

A small site-museum by the gate contains some good finds in a muddled display. Despite the crowds of visitors, this place still gives a feeling of wonder.

Norham Castle   Norham and its district were probably given to the monks of Lindisfarne by Northumbrian kings of the seventh century AD and belonged to the monks for a thousand years, long after their move to Durham (see Holy Island, page 115). The fine village church is like a piece of Durham Cathedral.

The castle was built on a steep cliff commanding a ford on the Tweed, when the border was being sorted out and was a stronghold of the Earl Bishops of Durham: Norhamshire together with Islandshire was not considered part of Northumberland, but of the County of Durham 60 miles (96 km.) away.

The remote and peaceful atmosphere of this beautiful place makes it hard to realize that the castle was besieged or captured by the Scots in 1136, 1138, 1214, 1318, 1319, 1322, 1327, 1463, 1497 and 1513, but the whole mass of patches, repairs and alterations makes it very clear. The inner ward contains the Norman Keep of *c*. 1160, much repaired in the 1420s, and badly damaged by the Scottish gunners in 1513, together with the lower parts of the domestic buildings. The outer ward contains fragments of two earlier gateways, but the defences date from 1513–15 and are a remarkable example of early gunnery-defences. One of the bastions was rebuilt as a fine Gothick lodge in Regency days.

Warkworth Castle   Warkworth Castle stands high above the fine little town, with a main street dropping sharply to the large Norman church and fortified bridge. Massive earthworks may date from *c*. 1140, when Prince Henry of Scotland was Earl of Northumberland. The gatehouse and several towers date from *c*. 1200 and there are various remains of the thirteenth and fourteenth centuries; Warkworth came into the hands of the Percies in 1332. Most of the character of the castle dates from the time of the second Earl of Northumberland (1416–55) who built the great tower-keep, reconstructed the hall, and began a large church across the middle of the castle.

The church was to have a central tower and transepts, and the foundations were laid with a vaulted passage built straight through under the altar and a vault beneath the rest of the chancel, but the scheme seems to have been abandoned at floor level. The hall has a magnificent porch-tower carved with a gigantic lion, the Percy crest, but the tower-keep gives Warkworth its unforgettable impact. The walls stand complete, and part of the roof has been replaced, topped by a high look-out tower. With marvellous skill, a whole large

manor-house has been wrapped up with its hall, kitchen, chapel, cellars and half a dozen private rooms into a fantastic carved block, the 'apogee of formal design'. Two centuries later the Cavendishes copied the idea at Bolsover (page 55).

Hadrian's Wall

Introduction Hadrian's Wall runs across the far north of England for almost 75 miles (120 km.) from the Tyne to the Solway, and is perhaps the most spectacular monument to Roman power anywhere round the edges of the Roman Empire. A long central stretch of the Wall sweeps through the most magnificent moorland scenery.

As a military installation the Wall probably always created more problems than it solved, and it was updated and reconstructed on many occasions. Working out the dates and functions of the alterations has given pleasure to five generations of archaeologists. The wall can never have justified its cost and must have been built largely to keep the troops busy. The whole scheme was drastically changed while it was being built and it was abandoned less than ten years after it was finished for the Antonine Wall, another 75 miles (120 km.) further north. These vagaries are absolutely typical of military installations at all times. Army councils and commanders constantly demand 'updating' and 'rephasing' and they had their way here, as they so often do. Later, when it came to the crunch, the Wall was not much use for it was captured, thoroughly destroyed and rebuilt three times in two centuries, although it seems that two of these destructions occurred when the garrison was away fighting civil wars on the Continent.

In *c.* AD 80 there had perhaps been a temporary frontier here, but only as a brief stage in the long-term Roman conquest of the whole of the north of Scotland. In *c.* 120, after Scotland had been given up and there had been serious rebellions in the north, the Emperor Hadrian was consolidating a long-term frontier-policy all round the Empire. The first scheme was a line of forts (see Corbridge, page 121, and Chesterholm, page 122), the basis for a patrol line on the north side of the Tyne and down the Irthing. In 122–30 the Wall itself was planned under Hadrian's own direction. It was built along the northern lip of the valleys with a small defence post—a milecastle—every mile and a small turret at precisely every third of a mile. Before this was finished at least eight large forts (including Chesters, page 120, and Housesteads, page 122) were built into the Wall and the aggressive potential of the line vastly increased by this extra manpower. It must have been extraordinarily frustrating for an able commander to be tied down on patrol duties based round the Wall, knowing that a single Roman cohort could go out and break up almost any opposition.

At this same period a large ditch, the 'vallum', was dug not far behind the back of the Wall, a strange piece of 'double-think' to mark the back of the military zone.

Very interesting recent work has made it clear that there was already a good deal of native cultivation on the line of the Wall. The relations between the local people and the garrison are receiving some fascinating research. Between AD 139 and 211 there was a lot of coming and going. Southern Scotland and the Antonine Wall were occupied and abandoned several times while Hadrian's Wall was put into 'mothballs', reconstructed and massively destroyed. Corbridge became a great supply base. From 211 to, very roughly, 400, the Wall and a series of distant outpost forts formed the northern frontier of Britain and, in the long term, were ineffectually maintained with ever decreasing resources. In the early days there was Spanish cavalry at Chesters and Belgians at Housesteads where later a unit from Holland was posted. Other troops came from Morocco, Syria and Iraq. Roman forces were posted very widely round the Empire. We know much less about units and organizations in the last centuries.

The Roman sites along Hadrian's Wall are quite difficult to understand, and foundations with a lot of complicated changes are not usually very attractive. The plans in the official guides need a lot of hard work since they often show things that have been covered up or things that probably exist underground but have not been dug up, while modern surroundings and harsh fencing are sometimes obtrusive. None of this detracts from the astounding impact of the Wall, however, and the bleak grandeur of the central section leaves an unforgettable memory. The visitor should not miss other remains looted from the Wall and its forts. There is a row of great pillars put up in Chollerton Church in Norman days. At Denton in Cumberland the chancel-arch was probably taken from Birdoswald Fort. At Corbridge Church the great tower-arch seems to be completely Roman and at Hexham Abbey, where there are many Roman carvings, the Saxon crypt is all of Roman worked stones, pulled off buildings at the great Corbridge base, and slotted together like children's giant building bricks.

What legacy did Hadrian's Wall leave behind, in the days when Roman authority had broken down and the Empire had disintegrated? Local people must have had a great deal of mixed blood, for Roman soldiers came from all over Europe, North Africa and the Near East. When the army had gone they were under Anglian chiefs and the kingdoms of Northumbria stood, in the worst of times in the Dark Ages, as a bulwark of civilization. At one end of the Wall, within the ramparts of the advance fort at Bewcastle, stands a great sculptured Christian cross, a work of art of *c.* 670–700 which, with its pair at Ruthwell in Dumfriesshire, is unrivalled in Europe. Just across the Tyne from the other end of the Wall the great scholar Bede (673–735), a monk of Jarrow, wrote the *History of the English Church and People* which made him the founder of English history. These works in the shadow of Hadrian's Wall show that there was something left after the whole defensive system had crumbled.

Description of the Wall   Construction of the Wall began in the east and worked west from Newcastle to Carlisle, and the numbering system that has been given to the milecastles and turrets runs from east to west, so it is best to describe the remains in that order.

The first $12\frac{1}{2}$ mile (20 km.) stretch of wall is disappointing, like the other end around Carlisle. All that can be seen out of three Roman forts, thirteen mile-castles and at least fourteen, if not twenty-five turrets, is *Turret 7b* (at $7\frac{2}{3}$ Roman miles from Wallsend) and a few hundred yards of *the Wall in short bits*, scattered up the middle of the main road or beside it. Some lengths of the *ditch* (in front of the Wall) and the *vallum* (behind it) can be spotted well out of the built-up area. It is sad to see how modern development and road works over the last fifteen years have failed to keep and make a feature of the Wall remains. At Benwell, in the housing estates of forty years ago, this was attempted outside the fort, and there are a little *temple* with concrete altars and a *crossing-gateway* on the vallum, both looking rather lost. The rest, $12\frac{1}{2}$ Roman miles of Wall, ditch, vallum, the three forts at Wallsend, Newcastle and Benwell, the other mile-castles (except for one gateway in a private garden), the turrets and the roads are lost under suburban Newcastle.

The next $12\frac{1}{2}$ miles (20 km.) to the north Tyne climb steadily through fine scenery. The remains of the Wall itself were flattened for a military road right along it, built in the 1750s for strategic reasons in case yet another Scottish army struck south through Carlisle, as four had in the previous century. There are very few remains actually open to visitors in this stretch, but long lengths of *ditch* and *vallum* can be followed on either side of the road, which crosses the bumpy pasture fields over the forts at Rudchester and Haltonchester.

The new roundabout where the Roman Dere Street (the modern A68) crosses the Wall could have had an interesting layout of the Roman crossing. Of the fourteen milecastles precisely spaced at Roman miles 14–27, half have been dug into and several can be spotted, but of the twenty-eight turrets twenty-seven are under the road and only the last, *Turret 26b* (at $26\frac{2}{3}$ Roman miles from Wallsend), can be visited, staked out with a length of Wall, in a fine wooded setting sloping down to the north Tyne crossing. A few hundred yards above this there is *a short length of Wall* beside the road.

Chesters Roman Fort (Cilurnum)   At the north Tyne the road swings away from the Wall to its fine bridge at Chollerford, from which an alien tarred path lined with concrete posts leads in about 600 yards (500 metres) to the *Roman bridge*,

where both the Wall and its Roman road were carried across the river. One side of the bridge stands, imposingly built of huge stones, on the bank and the rest of the remains of the bridge can be seen sticking up in the river, especially when the water is low.

A great detour leads round to the other bank where the Wall is lost under pasture, but in the slope beside it remains of the military *bath-house*, a sort of recreational club, stand to a great height. This requires a careful modern reinterpretation. Above this, in a maze of stout wooden and wire fencing, are the remains of the *fort*, a cavalry base. About a quarter of the footings have been cleared, the central headquarters, the commanding officer's house, a slip of the stables, parts of some barracks and most of the gates and turrets have to be puzzled out, but the official plan must be used with caution. These interminable foundations are the most extensive display of a cavalry fort anywhere in the Roman Empire: with imaginative reappraisal it could easily be the finest, in its splendid Regency park setting.

Corbridge Roman Base (*Corstopitum*) South of this stretch of Wall, on a rise above the Tyne is a large Roman site which was excavated in 1201 (by order of King John), in many later centuries and especially in 1906–14, 1934–9 and since 1946. Recent discoveries, under the bypass, have revealed a fort of Agricola's time (*c.* AD 80) a few hundred yards to the west. The actual site was occupied some time after by a new fort protecting the Tyne bridge and the line of Dere Street running north into Scotland, probably abandoned in 125 when the fort on the Wall at Haltonchester replaced it. Corbridge was re-modelled as a fort in 139 when the brand new Hadrian's Wall was 'mothballed' for the first time and the frontier moved up into Scotland, and there were re-buildings in 161, as inscriptions found there tell us. The place became a town and supply-base by about 211 and remained so until the end of the Roman period.

The remains on show are massive and extensive, but not easy to understand as they are only a fraction of a much larger Roman settlement. When the Tyne is low a good deal of the *Roman bridge* can be seen. Evidence for how the Roman place became the important medieval and small modern town next door is slight.

The 16 miles (25 km.) west from Chesters to Greenhead is the legendary and memorable stretch where the Wall runs on and dominates the high crags. For the first 6 miles (10 km.) the Wall is beneath or beside the eighteenth-century road and much has gone while the ditch and vallum are very complete. *Turret 29a* (at $29\frac{1}{3}$ Roman miles) and *a good length of Wall* look fresh from consolida-tion; further on *Carrawburgh fort* is a good bumpy pasture, beside which a track leads to a little *Mithras temple*, more happily sited in the open than the Benwell temple among the semis.

After the Georgian road swings away from the line *a long stretch of Wall* from *Milecastle 34* to *Turret 35b* is under a long-term clearance programme to within about $\frac{1}{2}$ mile (1 km.) of the Housesteads length.

Housesteads Roman Fort (*Vercovicium*)   The fort, built in *c*. AD 125 was added to the Wall very soon after it was built to command a natural line of approach through the crags. There have been very extensive excavations here over the last 150 years and Housesteads is one of the most completely known of Roman forts. The headquarters, the commanding officer's house, the two granaries, the latrines, a couple of the barracks and the walls, towers and gates are laid out. The rest—eleven long barracks and other blocks—have been covered over again. East of the fort a later *Roman gateway* was chopped through the Wall; to the west is *Milecastle 37*. Outside the fort something of the civil settlement, on terraces into the slope, can be seen and something of the roads and fields can be traced. The site and the setting are overwhelming—except when it is swathed in mist or when there is a steady downpour.

Chesterholm Roman Fort (*Vindolanda*)   This slightly older fort lies 4 miles (6 km.) south-west of Housesteads on the earlier patrol line. The headquarters and some of the defences can be seen and there is a very ambitious research project at work clearing the entire civil settlement, with displays and replicas.

Further along the steep crags from Housesteads *long stretches of the Wall around Milecastles 40 and 42* are under long-term reclamation and clearance. Close to Milecastle 42 round the Haltwhistle Burn and on Haltwhistle Common are many Roman practice or marching camps of which slight traces remain, and on the Wall there is little to see of Greatchesters Camp. There are further fine stretches of the Wall to be seen and *a good length at Walltown Crags* is maintained. Close behind the Wall are the slight remains of Carvoran Fort of *c.* AD 120.

In the next 9 miles (15 km.) from Greenhead to Walton, the Wall crosses the River Irthing and a great number of streams as it gradually drops into well-farmed land. A *number of sections* can be visited, all slightly in isolation, including the *Vicarage Garden* at Gilsland, many details around *Irthing bridge* (now on dry land beside the present river), a good deal of the Walls of *Birdoswald Fort*, and *three turrets, 51a, 51b and 52a* (which are $51\frac{1}{3}$, $51\frac{2}{3}$ and $52\frac{1}{3}$ Roman miles from Wallsend).

In the last long stretch of 25 miles (40 km.) through Carlisle to Bowness, there is nothing really to see. The devoted explorer can pick out a few short stretches of ditch and vallum here and there, and in a few places the overgrown mound of the Wall can be seen, but on the low coastal lands centuries of farming and robbing for building stone have caused almost complete destruction.

Beyond Bowness a chain of Roman watchtowers covered the coast of Cumbria against sea-raiders and recent finds suggest that a permanent ditch or rampart may have run some distance further.

Nottinghamshire

Mattersey Priory   These scant remains are of a monastery founded in *c.* 1185 for the uniquely English Gilbertines, who usually specialized in strictly segregated double-houses of canons and nuns. This establishment was for canons, and it was badly burnt out in 1279.

Rufford Abbey   The west cloister-range of a Cistercian abbey, begun in 1146. Bess of Hardwick (page 56) built some part of the great house that stood here later.

Oxfordshire

Abingdon County Hall   The hall was built as the centre of county administration for Berkshire, in 1677–83. There is a large room above, now a museum, and the lower storey is open as a market-hall.

Deddington Castle   These fine earthworks are of a castle of the local families

of Chesney, in the twelfth century, and the de Dives in the thirteenth. We must hope for a record of the excavations here.

Minster Lovell House   The whole establishment of a great medieval lord can be appreciated here in beautiful seclusion beside the Windrush. We can see the hall, the church and the estate buildings of the early fifteenth century (only here and at Tattersall and Wingfield can we see the whole setting of a late medieval courtier's house). The royal hunting forest of Wychwood was the great attraction and it is surprising that there are not more noblemen's houses in the district. The ninth Lord Lovell, Chamberlain of Richard III's household and Chief Butler of England, disappeared after Bosworth Field. Local tradition holds that, having escaped to Minster Lovell, he died there in hiding and that his skeleton was found seated at a table when a hidden room was exposed during building works. By the eighteenth century the house had fallen into ruins.

North Leigh Roman Villa   Early excavations in 1813–16, and others in 1910–11 and more recently, have cleared the whole main courtyard of a great country house, showing how it developed from a farm of the first century AD.

Rycote Chapel   This delightful isolated chapel survives from the earlier manor-house of the Quatremaynes and was consecrated in 1449. Most of the seats inside are original. The gallery, large family pews and the pulpit date from *c.* 1610 and the fine reredos from *c.* 1682.

Uffington Castle and
White Horse,
Oxfordshire

Only a small section of the great Tudor mansion of Lord Williams survives, but details of the moats and gardens can be glimpsed on private land. The lost medieval villages of Great and Little Rycote must be close by

Uffington Castle and White Horse   This large Iron Age camp is on the edge of the Downs; the famous horse cut into the turf below has been reckoned both Iron Age and Anglo-Saxon in date. Great fairs were held in the castle from the seventeenth to the nineteenth centuries to mark the fairly regular 'Scouring of the White Horse'.

Waylands Smithy, Ashbury   A long barrow which has recently been excavated and found to have been a small barrow without stone chambers, onto which a new end was later built with a substantial cross-plan burial chamber.

nster Lovell House,
fordshire
   The monument was substantially reconstructed in the 1960s.

Shropshire

Acton Burnell Castle The worldly and covetous Bishop of Bath and Wells, Robert Burnell, was Edward I's Lord Chancellor. In *c.* 1280–90 he built this very interesting block, part castle, part manor-house, part palace.

Langley Chapel, Acton Burnell A Tudor chapel.

Boscobel House and White Ladies Priory Boscobel House is a small Jacobean house, once hidden in woodland, and celebrated for its part in Charles II's escape from the Battle of Worcester in 1651. Nearby is the Royal Oak, descended from the actual tree in which Charles hid. Also concerned in the escape was the nearby mansion of White Ladies. This has disappeared, but the ruins on which it stood still survive as a small church of Augustinian canonesses, built at the end of the twelfth century. The romantic story has attracted visitors to Boscobel since the seventeenth century, but the custom of sporting a sprig of oak has almost disappeared. Oakapple Day, however, commemorated King Charles' birthday, 29 May, and not the days of the escape, 6–7 September 1651.

Moseley Old Hall, where Charles II spent the next two nights, is also open regularly.

Buildwas Abbey A fine ruin of mostly Norman buildings near the Severn, Buildwas was first Savignac in 1135, then Cistercian. The chapter-house is still vaulted and the shell of the church complete.

Haughmond Abbey An Augustinian abbey of *c.* 1135, well sited with good remains of the cloister and subsidiary building, mostly of the thirteenth and fourteenth centuries. Little is left of the church.

Lilleshall Abbey Another Augustinian house which replaced a Saxon community in Shrewsbury with canons from Dorchester-on-Thames in 1148. A good deal of the church, chapter-house and dining-hall remains. (Fig. 2.)

Mitchell's Fold Stone Circle, Chirbury A prehistoric stone circle with a standing stone and other tumbled stones nearby.

Moreton Corbet Castle Ruins of a square tower, gatehouse and walls and the shell of a large Elizabethan house of *c.* 1580, in a rural setting.

Old Oswestry A fine large Iron Age hill-fort.

128

Wenlock Priory King Merewald of Mercia built a nunnery here for his daughter Milburg in *c.* AD 680. We should not underestimate these Saxon princesses: far off in Bavaria St Walpurg is still revered and carrying out well-reputed miracles among the people she converted more than 1,200 years ago. Milburg's nuns fled before the Vikings and the church was re-established as a minster in 1050 by the great Earl Leofric, Godiva's husband. It was changed to a Cluniac priory by Roger of Montgomery, a Norman who did not come over with the Conqueror only because he was left in charge in Normandy. His share was the county of Shropshire and the rapes of Arundel and Chichester, very much the same posts of duty and honour as de Warenne's (pages 108, 173). Montgomery gave his name to the Welsh county.

Of the church, rebuilt in the early thirteenth century, the south transept and a part of the nave stand to full height. The magnificent fifteenth-century prior's house is a private house. (Fig. 3.)

Wroxeter (Uriconium) Roman Baths The tribal fort of the Cornovii was a great hill-top fortress on the River Wrekin. The Romans carried out their normal policy of establishing a new capital nearby but, unusually, the site has not remained occupied in later periods. Only the small village and Saxon church of Wroxeter stand within the area of the Roman city, which has lately come into the hands of the Department of the Environment.

There were excavations in 1863, 1912–14, 1923–7 and 1936, and others have taken place since 1952. One large wall survives of the elaborate public baths, dating from *c.* AD 200, and the foundations of the rest are laid out with the various warm and hot rooms and cold plunge bath. There is a display of finds in a museum on the site, and other finds from Wroxeter are in the museum at Shrewsbury.

Somerset

Cleeve Abbey   Cleeve Abbey lies on the edge of a rather overbuilt village in good farming country below the Brendon and the Quantock Hills. This small, moderately prosperous Cistercian abbey was founded in *c.* 1190 by William de Roumare II, Earl of Lincoln, whose namesake and grandfather had founded Revesby Abbey in Lincolnshire.

The fine much-patched gatehouse leads to an outer court. The church, now completely demolished, is outlined in the turf, but the cloister-buildings are complete and give a fine sense of enclosure. The east range is all of the mid thirteenth century (re-roofed in the eighteenth century) with the long dormitory above, and sacristy, library, chapter-house, parlour, passage and common room. The common room, whose vault has collapsed, is a fine pleasant room beneath, with little sign of Cistercian austerity. A good deal of alteration was done in this range in the fifteenth century with the details carefully matching the thirteenth-century work, to give all the monks bed-sitting rooms.

The south range was completely rebuilt in the late fifteenth century, with a couple of two-room flats on the ground floor and a very fine dining-hall, with a superb arch-braced roof with angels above, beside a small office with important wall-paintings. Behind this range are the remains of the thirteenth-century dining-hall, with a magnificent tiled floor.

The details of the west range, which was rebuilt in the early fifteenth century, are not yet clear, as it is partly built into the modern farmhouse. The kitchen at the south-west corner and the latrines at the south-east corner of the cloisters have both gone, but are remarkably intact at nearby Muchelney Abbey (page 133). The chief impression given by these fine ranges is of a monastic life of great style but extreme chill.

Dunster   There are various remains at Dunster, including a stone cross, a packhorse-bridge and the market-hall of 1609.

Farleigh Hungerford Castle   Farleigh was a new castle fortified in 1370–83 by

Sir Thomas Hungerford, at the same time as his neighbour Sir John de la Mere was fortifying Nunney (page 136). Both sites were chosen because the existing manor-house was there, and both were rather disadvantageous, in a village, and near the bottom of a valley with no outlook. Nunney, however, was a small tower-house inside a wide moat, beside or astride the old manor-house, and is still surrounded by the village, and overlooked by the parish church. At Farleigh, Sir Thomas Hungerford simply wrapped his castle round the manor-house in stages, just as Lord Hastings converted Ashby de la Zouche (page 96) and Kirby Muxloe (page 97). This required a vast amount of levelling up above the stream behind the house.

His son, Walter, who became Lord Hungerford, held the estate from 1398 until his death in 1449. Recognizing the defects of his father's too casual choice of a site, he moved the village away and built a simple new church up the hill in 1443. The site of the village he used for an outer ward, with defences climbing up the hillside, and the old church became the castle chapel, with many family tombs.

The castle survived the Civil War without damage, since all the local commanders on both sides were Hungerfords, but was sold off by the last spendthrift Hungerford in 1686. The castle was largely demolished and heavily robbed in the eighteenth century, leaving only the chapel and the two northern corner towers of the inner ward, which stand up impressively behind the weak defences of the outer ward, so that at the first glance the castle seems fairly complete. It has been in guardianship since 1915.

Glastonbury Abbey The main abbey ruins, fragmentary but wonderfully evocative, are still run by a trust. If the state takes over we must hope not to be confronted with too many more foundations. Glastonbury's origins are lost in antiquity and Arthurian legend. Perhaps a church of the sub-Roman period survived into Saxon times, and the medieval monks looked back to a first abbot in AD 601. Excavations carried out in the 1950s may tell us more when a report is published. Glastonbury Tor and Beckery chapel have told us much. There is a museum in a Tudor house on the abbey site. The George and Pilgrims is the abbey guest hostel. In guardianship are the abbey barn and the tribunal, a courthouse of the fifteenth century refronted in the early sixteenth, with a display of finds from the nearby lake-villages of the Iron Age and other local finds.

At Meare more abbey dependencies can be seen: in state care is the abbey fisherman's house of the fourteenth century. This is surrounded by many intriguing earthworks. The great pool, where the fish were, was drained at the end of the eighteenth century and is now broad fields. The key to the fish house is kept at the very fine medieval manor-farm.

Only in a Glastonbury shop would we see *Floreat ecclesia Anglicana*, 'May the Church of England flourish'.

Muchelney Abbey The abbey was founded on a large island in the Somerset marshes—still beautiful flat country—at a very early date, perhaps in the seventh century AD. There are remains of an early church displayed, with a curious kind of swimming-pool effect, beneath the later church. This church and all the cloister-buildings are completely flat, laid out in the turf as foundations. The north transept extends under the churchyard fence to within a pace or two of the parish church, rebuilt in the fifteenth century just beside it. At the south-west corner of the cloisters stand a fine group of buildings, which show something of what is missing at Cleeve (page 130).

The great fourteenth-century kitchen seems to have been split in half in *c.* 1520, to serve both the abbot's household and the abbey. A fine ante-room or small dining-room for the monks is now a site-museum and above this is a superb abbot's parlour with a built-in panelled window-seat and a fine fireplace. Other rooms, clustering round the demolished abbot's lodgings, have

Over the page
Abbot's Parlour,
Muchelney Abbey,
Somerset

133

been much rebuilt in the sixteenth and seventeenth centuries. The latrines (*reredorter*) can be viewed, but much is hidden since they are used as a farm-store.

The village cross, the priest's house (National Trust, open only by appointment) and the parish church should not be missed. The barns of the two big farms, though rebuilt later, give a fine effect of the abbey as the centre of a working community.

Nunney Castle In the middle of the attractive, rather muddled village, the castle comes as a delightful surprise, standing up proudly like a French chateau. It is a tower-house with all the parts of a manor-house piled up on top of each other, at once a romantic revival of a Norman keep and a workmanlike little castle with four large corner-towers behind a wide moat. It was built in 1373–83 by Sir John de la Mare, a minor local landowner, veteran of the wars in France, who was Sheriff and MP for Somerset and Wiltshire at various times.

The kitchen and store-rooms were on the ground floor, with servants' rooms, butteries and pantries on the first floor, and these two floors were much altered in Elizabethan times and given windows instead of narrow slits. The great hall on the second floor and private chambers on the third floor had wide traceried windows from the start, but it must always have seemed a bit claustrophobic living in such a small castle rising sheer out of the moat. The stables, farm-buildings and perhaps the old manor-house lay north and west of the castle.

The little castle was abandoned after a two-day siege in 1645; the north wall collapsed in 1910 and the ruins were placed in guardianship in 1926.

The handsome church with fragments of a Saxon cross lies on higher ground across the stream, and the old market cross, probably of 1259, stands beside the stream. It was rebuilt here in 1959, after an adventurous career. (Fig. 6.)

Stanton Drew Stone Circles ('*The Evil Wedding*') This important religious centre of the Neolithic and Bronze Age periods is too little known. Three circles, a stone-setting or 'cove', some rows of stones and a standing stone stretch for over half a mile (1 km.) in pasture fields. Seen at dusk they are not too suburbanized. Stanton Drew deserves the most skilful care, and the intriguing symphony in concrete and wire around the 'cove' should be taken down at once.

Staffordshire

Croxden Abbey A small Cistercian abbey started in AD 1176 with monks from Normandy. Parts of the apsed church and dormitory are quite well preserved, and the design of the apse was probably copied at Hailes Abbey (page 77).

Wall Roman Baths Astride the old line of Watling Street was probably, first, the headquarters of the Fourteenth Legion in *c*. AD 48–58, later a fort and in this a small town grew up. The town baths were dug up in 1912–14 and are laid out.

Suffolk

Burgh Castle Roman Fort The substantial outer walls of a coastal defence of perhaps the early third century AD remain. Saxon graves have been found near and there seems to have been an Irish monastery here in the seventh century. A Norman earthwork castle, which has gone, shows that this remained an important centre until the twelfth century. Little is known of this place. What was a cavalry regiment doing here? How large was the Roman town outside?

Doctissimis Viris
Societatis *Antiquariorum* Londinensis
PRAESIDI & SOCIIS
hanc Ichnographiam Eccles. Monasterij S.^{ti} Edmundi
quam ab interitu vendicavit Jac. Burrough A.M.
ejusdem Societatis & Coll. Caio-Gonvill. Cantab. Socius
D.D.D. Ol. Battely

Tota Ecclesia cum Campanili & Choro & Capella
B.ae Mariae Virginis longa est pedes 513.
Lata est à Porta Brachij Meridionalis ad Portam
Septentrionalem oppositam pedes 223.

I. Burrough delin. 1718.

Bury St Edmund's Abbey One of the earliest sites of Christianity in East Anglia, a church was founded here in AD 633 by King Sigibert. The last king of the East Angles was martyred by the Danes in 870; in 903 his remains were brought here and in 945 a vast endowment of neighbouring lands was given to the re-established community by the English King Edmund.

Bury St Edmund's became one of the wealthiest Benedictine abbeys in England and the early Norman church was laid out on a vast scale, 530 feet (150 metres) long. Only the west end of the abbey church stands above ground built to an extraordinary width by Abbot Anselm (1120–48). The badly robbed foundations of the rest of the abbey church are closely fenced in with wire and are unimpressive. Many of the buildings of the abbey precinct can be traced, including two impressive gates to the precinct, St James's Gate of 1148 and the Great Gate of *c.* 1330–80. (Fig. 2.)

Framlingham Castle A very powerful private castle where Roger Bigod, founder of Thetford Priory (page 111), was first installed by Henry I in AD 1100. For 200 years the Bigod Earls of Norfolk had an unmatched career of turbulence, treachery and rebellion. The castle walls date from the first Earl Roger's time between 1178 and 1213. His son Roger II became Earl Marshal through his mother. At the Conqueror's court the marshals had been subordinate officials who saw to the hounds under the constables, who commanded the bodyguard and looked after outdoor matters. Roger III was not on the best of terms with Edward I and made his contribution to the Welsh Wars by rebuilding Tintern Abbey and adding a lavish suite of reception rooms at Chepstow Castle (page 194) which he had inherited with the post of Marshal.

Through the Mowbray Dukes of Norfolk Framlingham and the now hereditary post of Marshal passed in 1476 to the Howards, who fell at Bosworth, were victorious at Flodden, and escaped the axe by a hair's breadth. Queen Mary was at Framlingham when she was confirmed in the throne, but after this the castle was abandoned and sold.

The earthworks of the outer bailey are clear, but there is nothing much within the walls.

Herringfleet Priory The remains of a small Augustine priory, started in AD 1216.

Leiston Abbey These are the ruins of the church and cloister-buildings of a Premonstratensian abbey, moved here in 1363 but founded nearby in 1182 by Ranulf de Glanville. He was Henry II's Justiciar, who captured the King of Scotland in battle and died on crusade in Acre.

Lindsey Chapel   A chapel of thirteenth-century date, set up for the adjoining castle.

Orford Castle   The castle was built by Henry II in 1165 at a cost of £1,413 9s. 2d., as precisely recorded in the Pipe Rolls. This was a very large sum for the period when the basic revenue of the Crown was probably less than £10,000 a year. Orford played a crucial role in maintaining royal authority in East Anglia and also commanded the important harbour of Orford, which is now blocked by the long spit of Orfordness.

The outer defences and buildings of the castle survive only as earthworks, but the extraordinary keep is complete—cylindrical with three large square projections. The general form of the keep was followed by a number of castles such as Conisbrough (page 173) and Pembroke, and a generation later there was a vogue for cylindrical keep-towers in South Wales. From the battlements there is a fine view of the sea and the Suffolk marshes.

Saxtead Green Windmill   A fine windmill, in working order. The top part, which goes round, dates from 1854.

Surrey

Farnham Castle   The round 'keep' enclosing the motte of a castle of the Bishops of Winchester, which was restored after the Civil War and is mostly still occupied. (The bishops' palaces at Bishops' Waltham (page 77) and Winchester are in state care.)

Waverley Abbey   Some thirteenth-century walling stands of the first Cistercian abbey in England, founded in AD 1128. There are parts of the south ends of the east and west cloister-ranges, and bits of the transepts. Excavation and clearance are proceeding.

Sussex

Bayham Abbey   Two unsuccessful monasteries of the 1180s combined in *c*. AD 1208 to open up a wooded property. Their buildings show that the very simple aisle-less early church, dormitory and west cloister-range were built first and the dining-hall later, perhaps by *c*. 1250. In *c*. 1260 the east end of the church, although far from old, was torn down, and a large new chancel and transepts built much further east. Parts of the church stand fairly high, and the gatehouse is quite complete. Cardinal Wolsey abolished the abbey in 1525 to endow his short-lived Oxford College, which Henry VIII in turn closed down in 1530.

141

The ruins were pulled about by Humphrey Repton to make them more picturesque for the Pratt family, whose head, Lord Camden, developed Camden Town in London, where we find Bayham Street, Pratt Street and Camden Road.

Hurstmonceaux Castle   A large brick show-castle of the 1440s, now the headquarters of the Royal Observatory.

Pevensey Castle   A Roman coastal-fort was built in the third century AD to secure a small haven, now silted and reclaimed. The fort is not the usual square, but oval. In 1066 William the Conqueror landed here and made the fort his

first base. The badly ruined keep is Norman. Within the fort the walls and towers of the inner bailey were built in *c.* 1240 by Peter of Savoy, the Queen's uncle, to whom Henry III had given the castle. Later, with so many others, it came to the Duchy of Lancaster.

Tyne and Wear

Hylton Castle   A tower-house of the early fifteenth century.

Jarrow Monastery   Bede, the great historian, who was a monk here all his life, tells how the much-travelled Benedict Biscop came back to Northumberland from Rome and Canterbury to found Monkwearmouth in AD 674 and Jarrow in 685. At both places there are important remains to see of these famed centres of civilization, and at both recent excation has thrown a flood of light on these early days. The church is still in use and the chancel is a small chapel of the seventh or eighth century. A great church on the site of the nave was pulled down in 1782.

Under the Normans an enterprising Saxon monk restored a community here after the Vikings had dispersed the old, but the Bishop of Durham moved the monks to join Durham and reduced Jarrow to a cell. The fragmentary monastic remains are of this short-lived second monastery.

Tynemouth Priory   The wide curving market-place of the town is lined with fine Georgian houses leading up to the strong defences which cut off the headland. The cliffs drop to the sea on both sides.

There was a monastery here from the earliest days of Anglo-Saxon Christianity, traditionally *c.* AD 630. After 800 the monks were frequently attacked by the Vikings, but they persevered and kept up some sort of a stronghold until 1008, long after most of the early monasteries had disbanded. (See page 115 for an account of the monks of Lindisfarne and the wanderings which led them to Durham, a site of equal defensive strength.) Nothing of the church or fortress of the Anglo-Saxons can be seen. An attempt in early Norman days to re-establish monks here as an annexe, first of Jarrow and then of Durham, was followed by a new foundation in 1090 by the Earl of Northumberland with monks from St Albans.

Tynemouth is a perfect ruined abbey with some fine upstanding remains and not too many confusing foundations laid out in the turf. The fine east end of the church (early thirteenth century) stands to its full height above the foundations of the earlier apse. A small chantry chapel of the period with ornate vaulting projects towards the east (mid fifteenth century). The west end of the church (mid thirteenth century) is half complete and most of the rest has gone.

Tynemouth Priory,
Tyne and Wear: an
engraving of 1813

The cloister-buildings are marked out in terraces in the grass, but the east side, the dormitory range, can be picked out leading to the massive latrines, or *reredorter*, of best monastic pattern, which were built in the eleventh century and reconstructed in the thirteenth, just like the church.

Tynemouth Priory has a strangely businesslike flavour, with a working coast-guard station just beside the church and with the immensely powerful defences, which cover whatever remains of a prehistoric or Dark Ages stronghold. The Great Gatehouse, almost a castle on its own, was rebuilt in the 1380s, and the ramparts were reconstructed in the 1560s as earthworks to carry guns.

Warwickshire

Kenilworth Castle   This magnificent castle alternated between royal possession and powerful magnates. The estate was granted by Henry I to his treasurer Geoffrey de Clinton. The great keep may date from *c*. AD 1160, and in *c*. 1173 the castle was taken back into the King's hands, remaining a major royal stronghold.

In 1244–66 the castle belonged to Simon de Montfort, at first a favourite and then a bitter enemy of Henry III, who retook it after a bitter siege. Kenilworth passed down the junior royal line of Lancaster to John of Gaunt, who rebuilt the inner bailey on a palatial scale.

The castle was maintained as a sumptuous residence and Robert Dudley, Lord Leicester, modernized the keep, built a high block to match it and laid out a pleasure garden in the outer ward. Queen Elizabeth stayed for nineteen days in 1575. Like Caerphilly (page 185), Kenilworth had extensive water defences.

Wiltshire

Prehistoric Sites   Wiltshire has the most important prehistoric stone monuments in Europe, rivalled in interest only by the much earlier painted caves of southern France and the Pyrenees and by the standing stone monuments around Carnac in Britanny. Among the Wiltshire sites two stand supreme, Avebury and Stonehenge, 'the most Remarkable Antiquity of Great Britain' as it was called 300 years ago. These two well-known constructions seem to be the largest and most elaborate religious monuments ever constructed in Europe by prehistoric man. Around them lie great numbers of burial mounds and other sites.

It is a sad experience to visit them. Stonehenge must be the most over-peopled spot in the British countryside and the barbed wire fencing and concrete tunnels which the DoE have provided to control visitors show a tragic failure to understand what is needed to manage the area for recreation and information. All around, the lesser sites are being devastated by misuse of the land, ploughed up for large-scale barley farming, and only the last vestiges remain of many of them. A handful are as complete as they were 150 years ago when the great expanse of downland on Salisbury Plain was cut up for farming, as almost all the other lowland commons of England were enclosed. Even thirty years ago far more of them were complete than today and our generation has freely permitted the most devastating damage to the sites and to the whole landscape. The worst single occasion was in 1966 when a new road was cut quite near to Stonehenge across the centre of Durrington Walls, a great 'henge' earthwork of the same type as Avebury and even more extensive.

Avebury, Wiltshire, in 1724

We can ask more questions about Stonehenge and Avebury than we can answer. What sort of religion were they built for? For how wide an area were these the ultimate spiritual centre? Whatever kind of educational knowledge did the builders possess? Intelligent speculation has run riot and books have been published claiming Stonehenge as the work of the Romans (in 1655), of the Danes (in 1663) and of the Druids (in 1740), all equally wrongly. Recent attempts, which we must hope are a bit closer to reality, suggest that there were both earthly and heavenly deities, superseded by water-gods in later pre-historic times which might explain the abandonment of Stonehenge. The social structure of the region has been partly reconstructed from the distribution and relation of major and lesser sites and there seems to have been a development from small local or petty tribes in Neolithic times to much larger 'nations' in the middle Bronze Age. We think of some kind of priest-king and of social gatherings and ritual feasts. Perhaps some of the earlier timber circles that Stonehenge represents as a fossil were roofed feasting circles.

However, the archaeologists have still not yet studied and compared the areas enough. We simply do not know how the people lived. Was there already in these early times a fairly settled population, with arable fields along the river valleys where all later cultivation has been concentrated? Why was Salisbury Plain left uncultivated and Stonehenge unharmed while the lesser but comparable group of sites on the Upper Thames around Stanton Harcourt has been under plough since the Iron Age and the 'Devil's Quoits' circle flattened? Was it because the plain was always especially sacred or because the light soils were more productive under grass? All this will only be understood from detailed study and comparison of area with area, of Stonehenge with Carnac and some of the other comparable areas under prehistoric, Roman, medieval and modern farming practices.

Just to compare Avebury and Stonehenge and their regions with one another is remarkably instructive. Each monument and each group of sites are astonish-

146

ingly different. Both are on chalk, but Stonehenge lies at a relatively low altitude on the crest of a rise, Avebury in a broad basin at a much greater altitude. Stonehenge and its associated sites show no clear relation to the fair-sized River Avon which flows south to the English Channel, but all the major sites at Avebury lie close by the headwaters of the Kennet, running east to the Thames and the North Sea, and this suggests that it was a sacred stream.

Both groups have huge 'henges' or gathering-places with the great banks outside and the ditch inside. Both have avenues and great stone circles. At

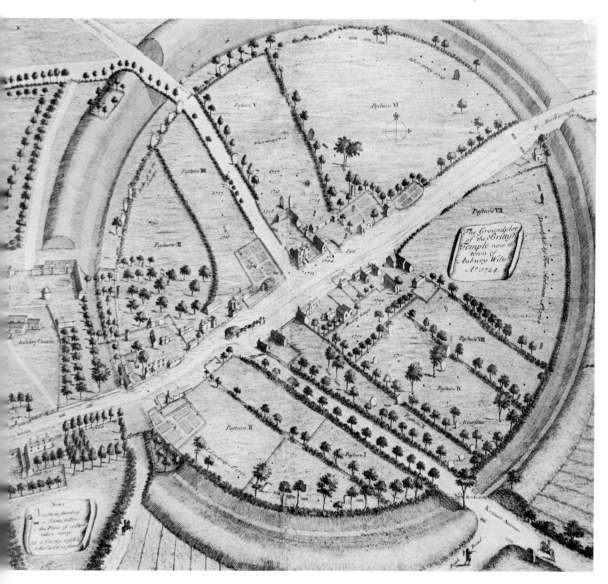

Stonehenge the stone circles are concentric, built of vast shaped stones, and lie well away from the great henge at Durrington Walls, while the avenue is simply banked and ditched. At Avebury the stone circles are not concentric, are of huge unshaped stones and lie within the great henge, while the avenue is of pairs of great standing stones. All the stones of Stonehenge have been brought there, the 'blue-stones' from South Wales, and the great 'sarsens' probably from near Avebury, but at Avebury all the stones are local. Stonehenge has a long embanked 'cursus', Avebury the gigantic man-made Silbury Hill. Both monuments have attracted a great deal of scholarly observation, too little of which has been published, and both have generated a mass of speculation of which all too much is in print. Stonehenge is now generally accepted as having an astronomical significance, but not Avebury. And no one has yet suggested that the whole of Avebury was roofed.

But what do these amazing groups really mean? Were they the joint or successive centres of a great cult or chiefdom? Or were they rival centres? Did they dominate the whole of England or were they only of local importance? And why did they survive? It may have been because they were respected and even used as sacred places for centuries after their main use or they may have been left simply because a predominantly pastoral economy did not demand their ploughing-up. None of these questions can ever be answered adequately by the kind of evidence that we uncover, and we will never know the answers. But a careful analysis of the forms and relationships will be able to tell us a good deal about the sites. Their relation to a developing rural economy in Neolithic and Bronze Age times, their relation to the trackways and ridgeways and their relation with lesser sacred or gathering sites such as Stanton Drew (page 136), Knowlton (page 63) or the Devil's Quoits in Oxfordshire are all fields with vast scope for original work. Another intriguing subject is the connection of the Ordnance Surveyors' planning with Colt Hoare's barrow-excavations and how far the excavations were carried out under the threat of destruction after the enclosing of the downs.

The Avebury Region One of the largest long barrows known, *West Kennet Long Barrow*, must be a communal burial place used for a long period between about 4000 and 2500 BC. The broader east end has a facade of huge sarsen stones blocking the five-chambered burial vault, from which forty-six burials were recovered in recent excavation and reconstruction. The pavement-lights in the roof of the central passage give a sombre lighting to explore the haunted side-chambers. It is strange that these very large monuments to the dead seem to be the earliest remains of a struggling population of cultivators. Beneath the nearby South Street long barrow plough furrows from the earliest days of settled cultivation have been found.

The National Trust's *Windmill Hill* is a 'causewayed-camp', a hill-top enclosure, of the cultivators who built the long barrows, which was occupied between 3600 and 2300 BC. It is not at all clear how they used these camps. The ditches have many gaps and they seem to have no value for defence. The three widely separated lines of ditch and bank seem to contain no permanent settlement, and the place may have been used for cattle round-ups. Hearths and debris in the ditches suggest that the people sheltered there at intervals for a few days at a time. A group of later round barrows show that the hill-top was used for burial after the 'camp' had gone out of use.

A vast conical mound, the largest in Europe, *Silbury Hill* was built perhaps as a memorial between 3000 and 2000 BC. A number of tunnels have failed to reveal the reason why Silbury was constructed, but the most recent has provided much biological evidence, insects from the old ground surface and even the grass still green after more than 4000 years sealed under the mound.

At *Avebury* itself, a gigantic circular gathering-place was constructed somewhere between 2700 and 1700, not as a stronghold since the bank is outside and the ditch inside. There are four entrances to north, south, east and west, and within the ditch stands a great circle of about a hundred huge sarsen stones, a rough circle which may follow a subtle geometrical scheme. Within this circle

Over the page
Avebury, Silbury Hill
and West Kennet
Long Barrow

149

stand the remains of two lesser circles of thirty and thirty-two huge stones. Each circle is the size of the whole of Stonehenge, more than three times the diameter of the largest 'blue-stone' circle there. In these two circles were smaller settings of more huge stones.

From the southern entrance an Avenue of a hundred pairs of large stones ran about 1½ miles (2½ km.) south-eastwards along a dry valley to the 'Sanctuary', on a hill above the Kennet. The Avenue is partly reconstructed and can be seen at the roadside. The 'Sanctuary', now on the A4, is reached from a layby opposite a transport café and is now eight rings of concrete stumps inside a wire fence. Some imagination is needed to see it as a double ring of stones, the outer circle a good deal larger than the outer circle at Stonehenge. This double circle was destroyed 150 years ago and the modern excavators also found six rings of post-holes left by at least three successive earlier wooden circles and multiple circles. The inner circles at Avebury, the Avenue and the Sanctuary in some form all seem earlier than the main gathering-place itself.

The Anglo-Saxon church just outside the main bank is worth careful study and the visitor should notice the earthworks of the medieval village-crofts across the centre of Avebury, which are prominent on air photographs and the ground, but are not mentioned in the guidebooks. Is the church just outside the monument because of a feeling of conflict between Christian and older sentiments? Was the Saxon village outside too and deliberately moved to occupy the monument in Norman times? The Roman setting of the monument deserves careful study and a main Roman road runs along the A4. Medieval and later documents can be used to tell us much more about the prehistoric remains. The present road along the Avenue was made between 1794 and 1815, when much of the damage to the stones must have been done. The earlier lane ran along the flank of Hackpen Hill and passed a group of barrows and another destroyed stone circle 350 yards (400 metres) north of the Sanctuary: is this an ancient route?

The finds from Avebury and the Avenue are in Avebury Museum. The finds from the Sanctuary are in Devizes.

The Stonehenge Region Stonehenge lies on one of the broad chalk ridges that make up Salisbury Plain. The ridges are separated by six fair-sized streams which meet within a few miles of Salisbury to make up the Wiltshire Avon. In their sheltered valleys, the population and the cultivation of the region must always have been concentrated. The ridges broaden and rise from a height of 350 feet (100 metres) near Salisbury to the high crest of the escarpment above the Vale of Pewsey at 700 feet (200 metres).

In historical times—the last seven or eight centuries—the fringes of the high chalk have been continuously under plough from the villages along the valley and the central strip was left as open downland. Between 1790 and 1830 the

16 The Stonehenge area: (1) Stonehenge, (2) the 'Avenue', (3) the 'Cursus', (4) the great gathering place of Durrington Walls and 'temple' of Woodhenge, and hundreds of prehistoric burial mounds, especially at Rattya (5) and Winterbourne Stoke (6). Settlement and cultivation have always been concentrated in the valleys, since prehistoric times

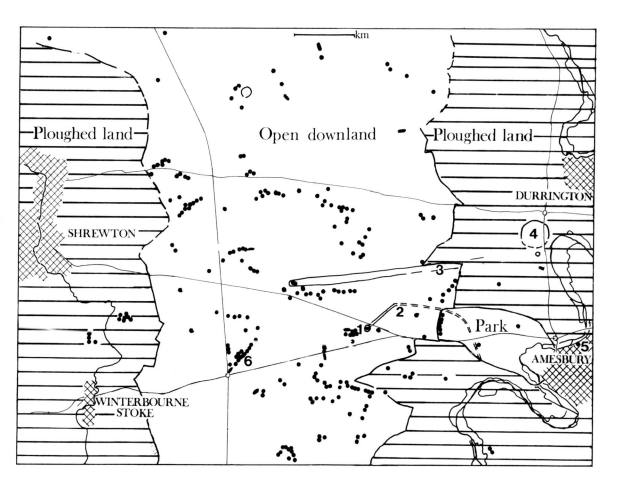

downs were largely enclosed into fields which, with the subsidies and machinery of the last sixty years, have been almost entirely ploughed up; fairly large areas seem to have been under the plough at times in the prehistoric period and Roman times. Usually the high chalk was best suited to grass and the only settlements were scattered farmsteads of upland graziers.

Ancient sites are irregularly concentrated and some areas of downland may be empty because they were reserved for grazing, others because they were still wooded. A balanced economic viewpoint is very difficult to sustain since almost all the thousands of early prehistoric sites are burial mounds with little to tell us about farming. From later prehistoric and Roman times we know of dozens of hill-forts, enclosures and farmsteads and hundreds of acres of field system, but they give us only part of an economic system of which the centres were always along the valleys.

The earliest remains of the relatively settled peoples are the long barrows—

great communal burial places used over a long period. West Kennet, near Avebury, is the most complete and accessible of the Wiltshire examples, of which seventy are known. Of the ten long barrows which cluster around Stonehenge, the most visible is dominated by the street-lights beside Winterbourne Stoke roundabout. Beside this a long straggle of later round barrows can be seen, many of them accessible (National Trust) and this pattern of a long barrow as the nucleus of a barrow group is quite usual.

The local equivalent of Windmill Hill (page 148) as a cattle-ranching depot seems to be the earthwork called Robin Hood's Ball on army land $2\frac{1}{2}$ miles (4 km.) north-west of Stonehenge.

The ridge of downs between the Avon and the Till was first marked out as specially sacred by the Cursus, almost 2 miles (3 km.) long and up to 700 feet (200 metres) wide, marked out with a bank and a ditch. This may have been for sacred games or ceremonies. Very little of the Cursus is left: for example, the west end is obscured by the overgrown debris of a First World War barracks and a later pig farm. The east end is not very clearly defined and only faint earthworks of the side banks can be traced. The Cursus points towards 'Woodhenge', a monument very reminiscent of the Sanctuary near Avebury. Although marked by the first Ordnance Surveyors in 1810, it was lost until 1925 and has since been cleared and reconstructed. It now consists of six rings of concrete stumps set in the old post-holes surrounded by a wire fence. There are only slight traces of the ditch, with a bank outside, and it is not easy to pick out the single entrance to the north-east. This entrance and the whole axis of the monument, which seems to be laid out on a subtle egg-shaped plan, points towards the midsummer sunrise.

Looking north from Woodhenge the visitor can see the much-flattened bank of Durrington Walls spanning the shallow valley in the foreground, a vast gathering-place of the Avebury type which seems to date from between 2700 and 1700 BC. The broad causeway of the modern road across it, a dismal piece of official vandalism, gave rise to extensive excavations which revealed signs of more great timber circles. Some archaeologists think that they were roofed as 'feasting-places', others that they were simply open holy places, with the posts perhaps carved like totem poles.

Stonehenge is the most extraordinary of all these sites and lies in the centre of the densest concentration of the early burial mounds. It is perhaps the most famous prehistoric site in Europe and its obvious religious and symbolic meaning provides endless fascination; but its setting crucially lacks that sense of space and peace through which a medieval cathedral gives such spiritual refreshment and impact. The monument was first laid out, perhaps between 2300 and 1400 BC, as an outer ditch, a bank within this, a row of fifty-six holes immediately inside this and a tall standing stone, about 18 feet (5 metres) high, out-

154

side the monument. This is called the Heel-stone or the Friar's Heel. Later a double stone circle was put up of eighty or so 'blue-stones', a dull grey stone brought from the Prescelly Mountains in South Wales. Various other constructions and the import of the huge lighter grey 'sarsen' stones from near Avebury produced Stonehenge in its present form between 1700 and 1000 BC.

In the centre lies a great stone of sandstone, perhaps from Milford Haven in South Wales. Round this stood a horseshoe of five pairs of huge sarsens, each pair joined at the top by a great sarsen lintel. Round this stood a circle of perhaps sixty blue-stones and a circle of thirty great sarsens capped by thirty sarsen lintels.

The central horseshoe of sarsens points north-east to the midsummer sunrise over the Heel-stone and another fallen stone called the Slaughter Stone, and equally south-west towards the midwinter sunset. There is another pair of stones just within the bank and a pair of mounds which seem to have held stones which may have important astronomical alignments and value for farming as they seem to allow the seasons to be observed.

The fine church at Amesbury should also be visited. It has remains of an Anglo-Saxon cross from the important early nunnery.

Abbey Barn, Bradford on Avon   A magnificent monastic estate-barn built in *c.* AD 1340 for the nuns of Shaftesbury, grander in scale but less lavish than the great barn at Glastonbury. A collection of agricultural implements is being built up by the Wiltshire Archaeological Society, and the whole farmstead might develop as a living museum. The farmhouse and medieval granary have been bought by the Wiltshire Historic Buildings Trust.

The whole setting of Barton Farm demands careful protection from the creep of modern suburbs. Will they engulf it? Or can it be properly maintained as a recreational area with all its character?

A fine bridge of *c.* 1200 and the likely site of the mill are 350 yards (300 metres) to the south-east, and these should also be used to contribute to our understanding of this fine group. Could a start be made by taking down the spiky iron fencing and hacking up the concrete path to the barn?

Bratton Camp and White Horse   A large hill-fort clinging to the escarpment of the Downs above a White Horse which may be of some age.

Ludgershall Castle and Cross   A minor royal castle with a great ring of earth-work and some fragments of walling.

Netheravon Dovecot   A dovecot of the eighteenth century.

Old Sarum The great hill-top site of Old Sarum with its vast and impressive earthworks was abandoned for the present city of Salisbury seven centuries ago. There are commanding views over fine unspoilt country to the north and over the present cathedral and the busy growing city to the south.

There may have been a hill-fort here in Iron Age times. Remains of a Roman building have been found, and there was an important junction of Roman roads here. In late Saxon times Sarum became a powerful fortress against the Vikings, and took over some of the functions of Wilton, Wiltshire's old shire-town, $2\frac{1}{2}$ miles (4 km.) to the west.

Drastic changes were imposed by the Normans and more than half the area within the ramparts was taken over for a new castle and a new cathedral for the Bishop of Sherborne and Ramsbury (1078–92). The castle was drastically remodelled by Bishop Roger (1102–39) with a palatial residence very much like his palace-castle at Sherborne (page 65). After his downfall the castle fell into royal hands and was further strengthened. It takes up the whole centre of Old Sarum, and a good deal remains, almost perched on a high plateau.

The cathedral, too, was vastly extended by Bishop Roger, the most powerful man of his day, and altered again by his successor. The foundations are laid out, rather flat except for a massive crypt beyond the north transept. Scanty fragments of a second Norman bishop's palace remain to the north. Within eighty years the cathedral, cheerfully described as 'ruinous' by an ambitious building bishop, was replaced by the present Salisbury Cathedral, founded in 1220; the spacious grid-planned city grew rapidly and replaced the crowded hill-top town and its suburbs.

Old Wardour Castle The castle lies in a wonderfully romantic setting with tall cypresses round a trim lawn, a 'Gothick' pavilion above the lake, a fine grotto of 1792. Even the narrow modern approach road runs dramatically through tall young pinewoods. The Georgian mansion can be glimpsed in the distance.

The strange and powerful design of the castle, in the centre of all this beauty, plays strange geometrical games with fascinating logic. The double-towered façade rises to an immense height, with something of the appearance of Nunney Castle (page 136), but there the great hall merely takes up the second floor with private rooms over and service rooms beneath. Here the majestic great hall takes up the top three floors over the entrance, and the service and private rooms are packed with great ingenuity round a hexagonal courtyard. Permission to fortify the castle was obtained in 1393 by the fifth Lord Lovell and the inspiration for this virtuoso design must have come from his time with the English forces in France: there is a larger hexagonal castle at Concressault, near Bourges in central France, while the completely circular plan of the new royal castle

Abbey Barn, Bradford on Avon, Wiltshire

157

of Queensborough in Sheppey (1361–75) shows the same predilection for geo-metrical experiments. Lovell's grandson built a far more orthodox manor-house at Minster Lovell in Oxfordshire (page 125).

In Elizabethan times the castle was rehabilitated, like many others including Nunney, and the work was done in 1576–8 with remarkable sympathy by Robert Smithson. At Longleat in 1572–80, Smithson and Allen Maynard were skilfully wrapping a bland classicizing façade round a brand new romantic house of 1567–70. At Wardour Smithson moved doorways and windows round with gusto, inserted dozens of 'half-medieval' windows, and gave the main en-trance and the hall stairs fine new classical surrounds. Echoes of Wardour are found in later Smithson designs such as the Little Castle at Bolsover (page 55).

This luxurious modernized castle was badly damaged in two dramatic sieges in the Civil War. In 1643 old Lady Arundel held the place with her servants and twenty-five men against 1,300 Roundheads under one of the Hungerfords (see page 130), and in 1644 the Cavaliers recaptured it after a stalwart three-month defence. The castle was never repaired and the whole back of it has collapsed. Visitors have been carving their initials on the stonework since the 1680s, and an important group of the 1720s on a first-floor doorway suggests that a Roman Catholic chapel was being quietly kept up here. The castle has been in guardianship since 1936.

Old Wardour Castle, Wiltshire

159

Worcester and Hereford

Arthur's Stone, Dorstone   A Neolithic long barrow in rather battered condition
with one very massive burial chamber surviving, and perhaps more now lost.
Why are there fifty long barrows in Gloucestershire, but only two in the county
of Hereford? Did they choose sites more vulnerable to later agriculture in Here-
fordshire?

Goodrich Castle   Godric's Castle lies in the district of Archenfeld which was
conquered from the Welsh soon after the Conquest, and the castle still carries
the name of its builder, as at Barnard Castle (page 67). It has a fine commanding situation suitable for an earlier hill-fort above an ancient crossing of the
River Wye which has given its name to the village opposite, Walford or Welsh-

ford. The fine small keep seems to date from Henry II's reign, but the bulk of the castle was the palatial residence of William de Valence, half-brother of Henry III and Earl of Pembroke, as he rebuilt it about 1280–1300. It shows the organized layout, the inner and outer ward and barbican, of a typical castle of the period. The kitchen, great hall, solar, chapel and other chambers were ranged round the inner ward.

There is no car-park and the castle is a good half-mile walk from the village.

Mortimer's Cross Watermill, Lucton   A small stone-built watermill.

Rotherwas Chapel, Hereford   A private chapel of the fourteenth and sixteenth centuries.

North Yorkshire

Aldborough Roman Town   Aldborough village, most attractive with a maypole on the green and fine views to the Cleveland Hills, lies on top of a prosperous Roman town. There were excavations in the eighteenth and nineteenth centuries, but only tiny fragments are to be seen. The visitor walks past an agreeable site-museum and along some pleasant wooded bumps with stones, which are completely unintelligible as a display of Roman town-defences. A path leads off to a well-kept vegetable garden, which has two good mosaic pavements each under a neat Victorian summerhouse. It is a strange period piece, which gives no idea that they are both part of a large Roman house.

Recent DoE concreting, walling and fencing clash with the quaint and pleasant character of the nineteenth-century layout of the remains. It would be fascinating to understand the area from prehistoric times. The Devil's Arrows, three huge standing stones a mile to the west, show that there was a sacred centre here in *c.* 2000 BC. Are there henge-monuments of the Bronze Age and a river-fort of the Iron Age lost under later cultivation, as have been found along the Thames near the Devil's Quoits in Oxfordshire? Why does the Roman town lie aslant the Roman road at Aldborough? Is the Boroughbridge crossing of the Ure a later Norman bypass for the Great North Road away from Aldborough?

The whole village and its unspoilt setting offer a superb field for the study of ancient landscapes.

Byland Abbey   An extraordinary series of moves round the north of England brought Abbot Roger and his monks to Byland in 1177. They had started from Furness Abbey (page 50) in 1134, and for a time in 1143–7 had started building close to Rievaulx Abbey (page 169).

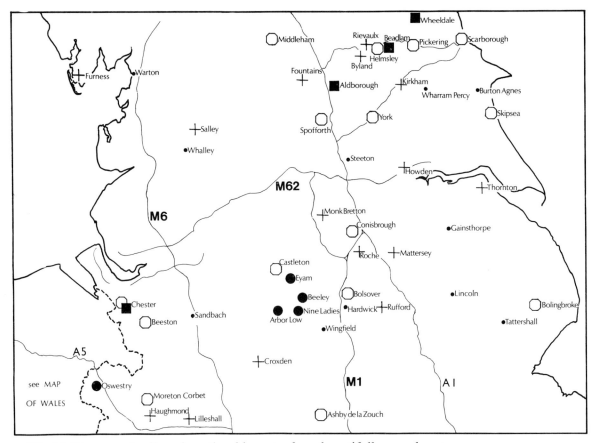

The idyllic pastoral valley where the abbey stands so beautifully was almost created by a long programme of reclamation and drainage: the monks built a series of dams and causeways, which served as roads to their outlying farms or granges, and drained the waterlogged land by diverting all the streams into a new channel which fed groups of fishponds, and powered watermills for grinding corn. This drastic transformation of the landscape as at Fountains (page 164) and Rievaulx was typical of the energetic Cistercians' treatment of the wilderness they sought. The result of their amazing skill and energy soon gave them the wealth and standing of a huge business conglomerate today.

Never as modest as their austere ideals, the Cistercians planned great churches from the start, 265 feet (75 metres) long at Rievaulx in *c.* 1135, 320 feet (90 metres) long at Fountains in *c.* 1138, and here the most ambitious of all was 350 feet (100 metres) long, a fair-sized cathedral scale. Byland, where the church was probably well advanced before 1177, resembles Roche Abbey (page 173) in its richly moulded and very French style and in the quality of its fine stonework.

162

17   Map of the north
of England. (See key
on Map 1 for types of
monument)

Byland Abbey,
North Yorkshire

Of the church the whole north wall, the west end and a corner of the south transept are standing. The chapels have early tile floors in patterns of fantastic geometrical ingenuity. The monastic buildings have been thoroughly excavated and parts stand to some height. The lay brothers' range dates from about 1160, long before the final move was carried out. Finds are displayed in a little stone site-museum.

Easby Abbey A constable of the nearby castle at Richmond (page 169) founded Easby Abbey in *c*. AD 1155, in the first years of prosperity under Henry II. He brought in Premonstratensian canons, a strict order of priests who were rather like Cistercian monks, but without their gift for propaganda and excitement. As at Egglestone Abbey (page 69) which was sent out from Easby, they did not plan ambitiously and the first church was about 50 feet (15 metres) shorter than the fairly modest Cistercian Roche Abbey (page 173). This church is mostly gone, but the cloister-buildings are very attractive, cleverly planned work of *c*. 1220–40 with new windows of *c*. 1300. North of the church the infirmary and abbot's lodging are rather later and less well preserved. The little parish church is also well worth a visit, and something of the workings of the estate can be gathered from the barns and mills which can be glimpsed.

Yorkshire has the finest abbey ruins in the country and Easby, very far from the wealthiest, stands among the most sublime. (Fig. 3.)

Fountains Abbey Fountains is the most complete abbey in the country, the very finest of ruins, and perhaps the best place in Europe to understand the emotional force of the early Cistercians. It was founded in dramatic circumstances in AD 1132–5 by a group of dissident idealists, monks from St Mary's Abbey at York, who soon joined up with the Cistercian order. The abbey grew with astonishing speed and within fifteen years had founded seven daughter houses. Gifts and endowments were showered on the abbey by north country landowners, unaffected by the religious turmoil of the times. At one stage the monks of Fountains caused an archbishop of York to be deposed, but his supporters retaliated by looting the abbey and burning it down. This was in 1147, towards the end of the long drawn-out civil war of Stephen's reign.

The early Cistercians were noted for farming knowledge and land clearance, and they used the direct labour of their hundreds of lay brothers for this work. By the thirteenth century Fountains was farming a great tract of land running from the abbey to Lancashire, from its own farms or granges. Wool was by far the greatest source of wealth and Fountains was the largest producer in the north and the richest Cistercian abbey in England. This commercial involvement was completely at variance with the ideals of the order, and later the abbey faced many difficulties.

The abbey buildings were built, in a plain but spacious style, in *c.* 1135–50. They were reconstructed and extended on an ever more ornate and immense scale in 1150–1250, but maintained with little change from 1250 until 1450. The great tower and the large windows in the church, the reconstruction of the abbot's house and other alterations date from 1450–1539 when the abbey was closed down peacefully and its great estates, worth over £1,000 a year, were sold off to speculators by Henry VIII.

The visitor is bemused and staggered by the vast ruins which he has to grasp on three levels. As architecture of the first order the long rhythm of the lay brothers' range and the church, complete except for the pillars and upper storeys round the high altar, vividly present the scale and organized pattern of Cistercian life. The major monastic buildings are an endless puzzle, a jigsaw or a detective story of change and function, an immense and unmatched complexity. With the lesser buildings, which are only partly cleared, we have to think in economic terms: the mills and bakehouses are part of the installations of a huge commercial empire.

The setting of the abbey was landscaped after 1768 when it was incorporated into the grounds of Studley Royal House. Excavations and repairs have been carried on since the eighteenth century, throughout the vast mass of building.

Helmsley Castle   The castle stands on a low rise with fine short views over wooded hills near Rievaulx Abbey (page 169). It stands where Ryedale and a number of other streams open out from the moors into the broad plain of Pickering, in a position of local tactical value.

Helmsley is a fine example of a local lord's castle, and its owners were the patrons of Kirkham Priory (page 166), a good way off to the south-east. The de Roos family held the castle in almost unbroken succession in the male line from 1154 to 1508. Behind a full ring of outer earthworks with stone-built barbicans of *c.* 1250 at each end lies the main circuit of walls of *c.* 1200 with round corner towers, a great tower in the centre of each long side and two gatehouses.

Kirkham Priory   An Augustinian priory was founded in the beautiful wooded valley here in *c.* AD 1125 by the Lord of Helmsley (page 166), some distance off. The canons prospered enough to send out a colony to Thornton in 1139, which soon became a rich abbey. This was at the request of the Lord of Holderness who held Spofforth (page 172) and Scarborough castles (page 169).

Very little of the early buildings remains. In *c.* 1230 the chancel and chapterhouse were rebuilt on a much greater scale. The rest of the cloister and lesser buildings were rebuilt in the late thirteenth and fourteenth centuries.

Middleham Castle   The fine big stone castle was started in *c.* AD 1170 by a

junior branch of the Breton lords of Richmond Castle (page 169), on a new site, more sheltered than the Norman earthworks which still command the junction of Coverdale and Wensleydale from higher ground. In this period new castles were quite often built away from their old sites, as at Montgomery (page 210).

The large and very complete keep dates from *c.* 1170–80, the lower outer walls from *c.* 1200–60, the chapel against the keep from *c.* 1260–80, the gatehouse from *c.* 1320 and the buildings ranged round the outer walls from the fourteenth and fifteenth centuries when the castle was held by the Earls of Westmorland, Salisbury and Warwick (the Kingmaker) and was later in royal hands. As so often the estate buildings, smithies, stables, barns and so on and perhaps a whole extra court of the castle have been pulled down. (Fig. 5.)

The little town of Middleham clusters attractively round the castle. It has lost many of its market functions to nearby Leyburn but is now famous for racing stables.

Mount Grace Priory There are extensive and interesting remains of this Carthusian monastery, the best in England of an extraordinary order whose monks lived in isolation in little houses under vows of silence. It was founded by the Duke of Surrey in 1398, long after the great monastic boom of the twelfth century. There were twenty-one comfortable little houses in two courtyards around the church, each with its own garden to grow vegetables. One of these houses has been reconstructed.

Richmond Castle   The great Lordship of Richmondshire was held by the Breton Earls of Richmond from 1071 to 1166. The castle stands above the town in a position of dominating natural strength, very suitable for a prehistoric hill-fort. The main wall of the castle seems to date from early Norman times, *c.* 1070–90, as does the main hall of the castle which stands high above the River Swale. The remainder of the buildings along the river front are of twelfth-century date. The keep, too, is of the twelfth century but incorporates the main early Norman entrance to the castle. The completeness of the early remains is remarkable and is only rivalled by Chepstow as the castle of a great lord in early Norman times. The entirety of the castle with the small grey town and the sweeping scenery is still little spoilt.

Rievaulx Abbey   This abbey was the first Cistercian house in the north of England. Waverley in Surrey had been founded in AD 1128 and in 1131 St Bernard himself sent out from Clairvaux his personal secretary as abbot with twelve monks. Two of the early abbots were recognized as Saints. By 1150 there were 140 full monks and over 500 lay brothers under vows, although four daughter houses had been sent out; it is as hard for us to understand this religious enthusiasm as it is to see why the Cistercians so savagely disapproved of the rich liturgy and architecture of the Benedictines and Cluniacs. From the very start they were just as politically minded and within two generations they were just as wordly. But the energy they unleased on their surroundings was devastating, and here they moved the river to the other side of the valley among other great farming and engineering works.

Mount Grace Priory, North Yorkshire

The lower part of the very plain transepts and scant ruins of the nave of *c.* 1135–50 survive in the church and there are some fragments of the early monastic buildings, but the whole impression of Rievaulx is given by the east part of the church (like Whitby Abbey, page 172) and the monks' dining-hall, both lavishly and grandly rebuilt in *c.* 1225–50. Unlike Fountains, which seems so much of a piece, Rievaulx has obvious signs of much more continuous reconstruction throughout medieval times. It is most dramatically sited against the side of a valley with fine wooded hills. Here, too, a Georgian landowner used it as a focus in his landscape.

A very large collection of carved stones is laid out and there must still be great ranges of storehouses, barns and workshops to be found. (Fig. 2.)

Scarborough Castle   The great coastal stronghold above harbour and town succeeded a Viking hill-fort from which comes the name 'Skarthi's burh', Scarborough. Before that a small Roman fortified signal station stood on the edge of the cliff and its outline can still be seen within the castle, close to where the Iron Age and Bronze Age settlement has been found.

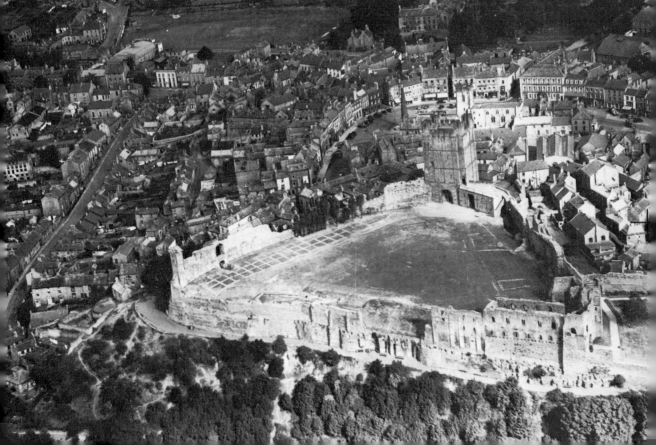

The fortress was in the hands of a local Anglo-Norman lord until taken over by Henry II, a great castle-builder, who held together an empire from the Tweed across half France to the Pyrenees. His concern for the east coast is also seen at Orford (page 141), but Scarborough's main function was more as a support and supply base for the Scottish border. Henry II's massive keep of 1157–69 and the similar one he built at Newcastle upon Tyne are very much younger brothers of his vast keep at Dover (page 87). The main outer wall dates from *c*. 1210 and reminds us that King John who built it was on notoriously bad terms with the northern barons. The sombre projecting barbican dates from 1243–5, but records for later years tell, as so often at royal castles, of slow crumbling and attempts at repair.

Scarborough had a long, dramatic and rather off-beat military history. A group of barons headed by the Earl of Lancaster, who then held Pickering Castle 15 miles (24 km.) away, besieged and executed the royal favourite Piers Gaveston in 1312. In 1318 the Scots burnt the town but avoided the castle. In Tudor times the castle had more than its share of trouble. It was held for Henry VIII against the Pilgrimage of Grace in 1536, and in 1557 a protester against Mary recklessly seized the castle. The great natural strength of the headland was shown in a long and gallant Royalist defence in 1644–5 and in 1648 the Parliamentary governor declared for the King.

Spofforth Castle Here are remains of the fourteenth-century hall with traces of the older castle of the Percies of Alnwick and Warkworth (page 116). Spofforth was slighted by the Yorkists after the third Earl of Northumberland's death at the Battle of Towton in 1461.

Stanwick Oppidum A short length of the vast defences of this Brigantian capital of the first century AD is open. A fine Iron Age sword is in the British Museum.

Steeton Hall Here is an intact fourteenth-century gatehouse of fine white cut-stone. Something of the moat and enclosure wall can be glimpsed and the farmhouse seems to be partly medieval.

Wheeldale Moor Roman Road Almost a mile of road of the first century AD can be seen near the Roman camps at Cawthorn.

Whitby Abbey The ancient abbey, founded originally by St Hilda in AD 675, stands high on the cliff above Whitby town and harbour. The Anglian monastery was a double house for men and women and became the burial place of the Northumbrian royal house. Here took place the Synod of Whitby in 664, to iron out the differences between Celtic and Roman influences in the Church. The church was sacked by the Danes in 867 and refounded in early Norman times. After the dissolution the monastic buildings were destroyed to build a residence. The nave of the abbey church collapsed in 1762; the south transept

in 1763; the west front in 1794; and the central tower in 1830. The standing chancel and north transept represent a thirteenth-century rebuilding of the Norman church and the design of the east end with tiers of three massive lancets is a characteristic north country design. North of the church extensive excavations in 1924–5 revealed widespread traces of the Anglian monastery, but the interpretation of the findings shown on the official guide is open to question. Many finds from the early monastery are now in the British Museum. (Fig. 3.)

Clifford's Tower, York Castle   A shell keep of clover-leaf plan, built on one of the two mottes in *c.* 1250, can be seen. York itself has innumerable treasures, and the walls, gates and houses need hardly be mentioned.

South Yorkshire

Conisbrough Castle   Dramatically crowning a hill above the industrial suburbs are the fine remains of the small royal castle. The tall, circular keep with broad buttress-like projections is well preserved, and copied from Orford (page 141).

Monk Bretton Priory   The priory was founded by a local notable in 1154, the first year of certain peace after the troubles of Stephen's reign. The monks were Cluniacs, who stood for pomp and lavish services, and came from the monasteries at La Charité on the Loire in France and from nearby Pontefract.

There is a good gatehouse and barn. The church dated from 1170, the east range from *c.* 1220, and the south range from *c.* 1280, to judge from the very little that remains. The west range was the prior's lodging of the fourteenth century, converted into a house in Elizabethan times. The guesthouse and infirmary are very flat.

The priory stands on the edge of a housing estate near Barnsley in the West Yorkshire Coalfield and the once fine valley setting is strewn with the paraphernalia of modern industry.

Roche Abbey   Roche Abbey was founded for the Cistercians in 1147 and stands within a few paces of the steep rocky face (which gave it the name) of a gentle and beautiful valley. Approach is by an immensely grand but ruined gatehouse, past a charming Gothick lodge of 'Capability' Brown's time. Most of the monastic buildings are laid out as foundations, but none of the barns or brewhouses have been found. The only part standing to any height are the east walls of the transepts of the church, which was built in the 1170s in an advanced style similar to Byland Abbey (page 161), but to a much simpler plan. The stonework is of the finest quality. (Fig. 2.)

It is sensible to avoid summer weekends in this beauty spot.

Wheeldale Moor
Roman Road, North
Yorkshire

173

Roche Abbey, South
Yorkshire

Early Prehistoric Sites

Beaumaris Castle ■

Conwy Castle

Rhuddlan Castle   Whitford Cross
St Winifrid's, Holywell   Basingwerk Abbey

Flint Castle ■

Ewloe Castle ■

(Segontium) Roman Fort   Caernarfon Castle

Gwydir Uchaf Chapel

Denbigh Castle, Town Walls ■

Dolbadarn Castle

Fedw-Deg •

Derwen •

Dolwyddelan Castle

Capel Garmon, Llanrwst •

Llangar ■   Valle Crucis •

Llangybi •   Crieieth Castle ■

Penarth Fawr •

Chirk Castle ■

Harlech Castle ■

Dyffryn Long Barrow •   Cymmer Abbey •

Castell y Bere •

Montgomery Castle ■

Dolforwyn Castle •

Strata Florida •

St Dogmael's Abbey ■   Cilgerran Castle ■

Pentre Ifan Burial Chamber •

Bronllys Castle ■

Talley Abbey ■

Brecon Gaer ■

Llanthony Priory ■

Grosmont Castle ■

St David's Bishop's Palace ■

Skenfrith •

St Non's Chapel

Llawhaden Castle •

Carreg Cennen Castle ■

Tretower Castle and Court ■

White Castle ■

Monmouth Castle ■

Raglan Castle ■

Llanstephan Castle ■   Kidwelly Castle ■

Tintern Abbey ■

Carew Cross •

Loughor Castle •

Chepstow Castle ■

Runston Chapel •

Bishop's Palace, Lamphey ■

Neath Abbey •

Caerleon ■

Weobley Castle ■

Swansea Castle

Margam Museum ■

Caerphilly Castle ■

Newport Castle

Caerwent ■

Parc le Breos Burial Chamber •

Coity Castle ■

Castell Coch ■

Newcastle, Bridgend ■

Ewenny Priory ■

Ogmore Castle ■

Old Beaupre Castle ■

Tinkinswood, St Lythans Burial Chambers

0   10   20   30 m
0   10   20   30   40
km

18   Historic monuments: Wales

Wales

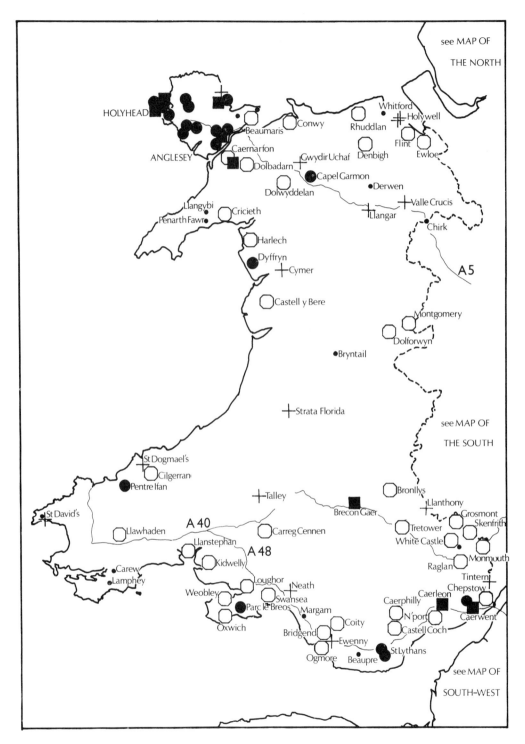

19 Map of Wales. (See key on Map 1 for types of monument)

Clwyd

Basingwerk Abbey   Basingwerk was probably founded by Ranulph Earl of Chester in *c*. AD 1131 for the Savignac order and dedicated to St Mary. The abbey remains are very fragmentary.

Chirk Castle   The fine iron gates are of *c*. 1720. The castle is the only one in North Wales of the time of Edward I that is still lived in.

Denbigh Castle, Town Walls and Churches   The castle stands up proudly on the rocks like a hill-fort. The castle and town just below were walled in 1282–94 by Henry de Lacy, Earl of Lincoln; Edward I gave him his lordship as part of his plan to subdue the Welsh. After its capture by the Welsh, rebelling briefly in 1294, Master James of St George was called in and started a Caernarfon-style inner line of wall, with the same wilful ingenuity. The magnificent three-towered gatehouse was never completed. It was much damaged in a sixth-month siege in 1645.

The contemporary town walls surround a small area below the castle and a borough was founded here in 1282. Much of the walls and one of the gates are still there, though the town has moved out into the valley below.

The town chapel of St Hilary survives only as a tower. The impressive shell of a puritan cathedral stands beside the chapel; Lord Leicester who entertained Queen Elizabeth so regally at Kenilworth (page 145) meant here to replace St Asaph's cathedral. Some ruins of the friary may also be seen below the town.

Derwen   A late medieval churchyard cross can be seen.

Ewloe Castle   This minute castle of the Welsh princes looks very indefensible lost in a wooded valley about 470 yards (400 metres) from the road. Two big towers and part of the walls are left.

Flint Castle   Flint Castle was built by Edward I between AD 1282 and 1294 on a rocky outcrop above the Dee as a garrison castle for £6,000 with the town walls. It is square with four corner towers, one grossly inflated and cut off as a keep. Flint lies in the great industrial zone along the coast, reeks of chemicals and lies beside a large factory and housing estate, which uses it as an adventure playground.

St Winifrid's, Holywell   An extraordinary complex of parish church, which is now Anglican, chapel beside it, which is state run, and below that an amazing medieval vaulted holy pool, in Roman Catholic hands.

Rhuddlan Castle This sublime and perfect garrison castle overlooks the Clwyd: was this saltmarsh, mud or water? The main ward of the castle is symmetrical in plan with double gatehouses and single towers opposed. The outer defences, little more than an edging to the moat, have smaller towers and command a dock at the rivers' edge.

Master James of St George built this and the town for £9,500 at great speed in 1277–82. The work included digging a new channel for the river: how did Edward's armies cross it and the rest of the mud flats?

Next to Edward's town and castle are the sites of a town and castle built here in the time of William the Conqueror, and the high castle-motte is in guardianship.

Valle Crucis In the 'valley of the cross' lies a small Cistercian abbey of the Princes of Powys, founded in 1201. Much of the church survives and the east cloister-range is complete. It is of the late fourteenth century, with many later changes. There is a fine inscribed stone to Prince Eliseg 470 yards (400 metres) to the north. Prince Cyngen, who put it up to his great-grandfather, died on pilgrimage in Rome in AD 854.

Whitford Cross   A fine tall cross of *c.* AD 1000 behind a fence in a field.

Dyfed

Carew Cross   One of the finest early crosses in Wales. This cross seems to be of early eleventh-century date and to commemorate the gift of an estate to the church. It lies by the entrance to the great ruined castle of Carew, which is still in private hands.

Carreg Cennen Castle   The castle on its precipitous hill-top, a real 'eagle's nest', may well succeed a hill-fort of Iron Age or Dark Age date. Quite remarkably the castle built by one of Edward I's henchmen, John Giffard, in *c.* 1280–1300, shows the ordered regularity of Edward's castles in North Wales. The elaborate entrance defences had a long barbican with three sets of drawbridges between the outer ward and the main castle. The gatehouse and the residential range of the inner ward where the chapel, solar, hall and kitchen of the domestic quarters can still be recognized show much of the character of Edward's work. From a corner of the inner ward a staircase descends to a long defended passage (now closed) which leads down to a cave running back 40 yards (35 metres) into the hill below the outer ward. The castle was 'slighted' and abandoned in 1662.

Cilgerran Castle   The castle stands above the superb wooded gorge of the Afon Teifi and may have been an early Welsh fortress. Most of the main defences of the inner ward seem to date from soon after 1223, when the place was captured by the Marshall, Earl of Pembroke, of the day, and the round towers copy that at Pembroke. Cilgerran remained a garrison castle of the Earldom rather than a residence, and the buildings within the inner ward are difficult to identify from the scanty footings. Very recent excavations have revealed remains of stables and bakehouses in the outer ward. (National Trust.)

Kidwelly Castle   The main part of the castle was built *c.* 1275 by Payn de Chaworth, one of Edward I's principal aides in the conquest of North Wales, on the site of the earlier castle of Maurice de Londres. Payn squeezed a miniature castle of the Harlech type within the earlier earthwork, which is semi-circular in plan. On the marriage of the King's brother, Edmund of Lancaster, to the heiress of the castle the domestic range within the inner ward was completed (*c.* 1300) and shortly afterwards the outer ward was given a stone wall

181

and great gatehouse, on a scale which made Payn's castle look ridiculous. During the fifteenth century, when the castle was a minor Crown possession, a large hall was built in the outer ward almost touching the walls of the inner ward.

Kidwelly is a double settlement with a 'castle-town' on the north bank of the River Gwendraeth. The line of the town defences can still be recognized by low earthworks and the fourteenth-century South Gate still stands. On the south bank, across a medieval bridge, the town has grown greatly around the priory church founded in 1115.

Bishop's Palace, Lamphey   Here are the extensive remains of a manor-house of the medieval Bishops of St David's on an ancient estate of the church, a few miles east of Pembroke. The buildings are of various dates between the thirteenth and sixteenth centuries and the earliest part dates from a generation or so before any part of the Palace of St David's. The official guide calls this a *camera*, but it is perhaps a hall, and the 'great hall' whose arcaded parapet closely resembles Bishop Gower's work at St David's should perhaps be identified as a low private gallery.

182

The lush rural setting is little spoilt by a few nearby pylons and council houses and by the small village sewage-works which backs on to the grounds.

Llanstephan Castle   One of the most beautiful and picturesque castles in Wales, Llanstephan still retains a superb atmosphere with fine views and sandy beaches on the Tywi estuary. The early history is obscure and the castle was often in Welsh hands. The siting is typically that of a promontory fort of the pre-Roman Iron Age which may await discovery beneath the castle. Most of the ruins date from the thirteenth century and the walled-up great Gate House is a close copy of Caerphilly Castle (page 185).

Llawhaden Castle   The substantial remains of a castle of the Bishops of St David's of *c*. AD 1310–20 can be seen.

Pentre Ifan Burial Chamber   Of a long barrow, the burial chamber and part of the forecourt remain on a spur of the Prescelly Mountains, from which the 'blue-stones' were taken to Stonehenge (page 152) in prehistoric times.

Bishop's Palace, St David's   An unrivalled group of medieval buildings still stands at the shrine of the patron saint of Wales, no doubt on the site of a Celtic monastery dating from the sixth century. The cathedral is still maintained by the Church and dates from the end of the twelfth century, with many later alterations and rebuildings. Both the Bishop's Palace and the remains of the precinct wall are maintained by the Department of the Environment. It is not clear whether the precinct wall which dates from the years around 1300 follows an earlier line. The wall and the palace were begun by Thomas Bek, Bishop of St David's from 1280 to 1293, a great reformer and magnate who was visited by Edward I at St David's in 1284. Bishop Bek's hall and solar form one side of the courtyard. Another side is formed by the very much larger great hall of Bishop Gower, Bishop of St David's from 1328 to 1347. The extraordinary arcaded parapet and chequer-pattern masonry is a local speciality, but the depressed ogee arches of the porch of the great hall and other elaborate details have parallels elsewhere in the west, as at Berkeley Castle. The palace seems to have been abandoned during the seventeenth century.

St Non's Chapel, St David's   By the edge of a rocky bay, three-quarters of a mile south of the cathedral, stand the foundations of this chapel, dedicated to the saint's mother. The chapel dates partly from the Celtic period. The fortunate visitor will be able to see the sun setting on a clear day.

St Dogmael's Abbey   On the site of a Celtic monastery at the head of the estuary

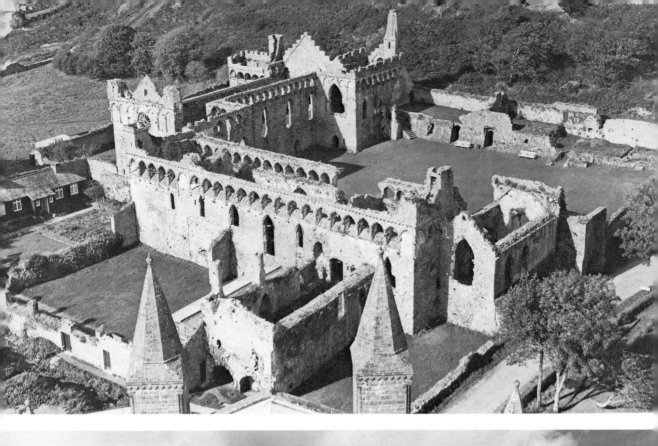

of the Afon Teifi, the abbey was founded in about 1115 by the local Norman lord. The community was part of the French order of Tiron, a minor centralized ascetic order like the Cistercians, who attracted far more attention in England. The site consists largely of trim foundations; parts of the church, the chapterhouse and the infirmary still stand.

Strata Florida A few remains of a small Cistercian abbey, first Norman and later Welsh, can be seen. As at Roche (page 173), the transept chapels have lasted best.

Talley Abbey The abbey was founded by the Welsh prince Rhys ap Gruffudd for the Premonstratensian order of canons, an evangelical organization which enjoyed a brief popularity at the end of the twelfth century. Records suggest many difficulties in the life of the abbey, and the buildings seem never to have been completed. Part of the central tower stands; the foundations of the church have been cleared, but the cloister-buildings lie under the adjacent farmyard. The site is one of beauty and silence.

Mid Glamorgan

Newcastle Bridgend The castle stands above a ford of the Ogmore river. There is a single walled enclosure with two square towers and a very fine ornamented entrance gateway. The domestic buildings within have been only partially exposed and from an early date the castle was not more than an outpost of Coity Castle (page 186). The pleasant atmosphere of castle, church and hamlet is at risk with the demolition of many of the nearby cottages.

Caerphilly Castle The great castle of the Clares dominates the small industrial town of Caerphilly, at the end of the mountainous country of the mining valleys. In Roman times there was a small fort nearby. The castle was built by Earl Gilbert de Clare after his conquest of the district from the Welsh in 1266, at first as a frontier fortress to protect his Glamorgan lands. The castle was conceived on an even grander scale than Edward I's castles in North Wales, with a great fortified dam and vast lake-defences. Before it was completed the independent Welsh had been conquered and the castle was obsolete except as a base for administration and putting down occasional revolts.

The inner ward contains the residential buildings. The great hall, largely rebuilt in modern times, with the ruinous state rooms is at one end and the kitchen, unusually sited in a great tower, to the side. The defences of the inner ward are of the well-planned Edwardian type with great corner towers and vast east and west gatehouses, each big enough to contain great suites of rooms. Beyond these defences a second ward is defended by fairly low battlemented walls, commanded by the inner ward. To the west a large hornwork and to the east the complex dam-defences form further lines of protection, with an outer moat to the east again. Much of the stonework is modern, but Caerphilly gives an excellent idea of the character of a medieval castle on the largest scale.

Coity Castle   The large residential castle of the Turbevilles and the Gamages stands in a straggle of modern houses. It lies beside the church and may stand on an early Welsh fortress.

Ewenny Priory   The lords of Ogmore Castle (page 187) founded the priory in *c.* 1120, probably on the site of an earlier Welsh foundation. The priory was a cell of the great Benedictine abbey of Gloucester which remained as the

parent house throughout the Middle Ages. The nave of the church dates from about the time of the foundation and is still used as the parish church. The crossing presbytery and south transept which have separate access, together with the ruined north transept, date from a decade or two later. The cloister-buildings have been demolished or incorporated in the present house, but the precinct walls still exist round more than half their length and are an unusual and impressive survival with three towers and two gatehouses. The siting is spoilt by three different cable lines and a concrete bridge nearby, with a couple of housing estates, a gas works and a caravan site on the skyline.

Ogmore Castle   The castle lies just above the mouth of the Ewenny river at an important ford where the river is still crossed by stepping stones. Ogmore is a small residential castle that was never reconstructed or developed in the late thirteenth or fourteenth centuries, as was the case with most Welsh castles. The only tower on the curtain of the inner ward is the small Norman keep. The domestic buildings are not incorporated into a regular layout but scattered about. The only significant addition of late medieval times is the court house in the outer ward to the west where the business of the lordship was done when it was in the hands of the Duchy of Lancaster in *c.* 1330. The fragment of a cross set up to mark the gift of land to the church, displayed on the site in replica, dates from a generation or so before the Norman Conquest. As with the cross at Carew, the Normans must have been overbearing in their dealings with the Church when strategic land was at stake.

South Glamorgan

Castell Coch   On the ruins of a little thirteenth-century castle, romantically situated in wooded hills on the outskirts of Cardiff, an extraordinary reconstruction of a medieval castle was built by the Marquis of Bute in the 1870s. Bute employed the architect William Burgess for his fantastic rebuilding of Cardiff Castle (1865–85) and Castell Coch served as no more than a weekend cottage or shooting box to that gigantic folly. At much the same time Ludwig II was constructing his dream castle of Neuschwanstein, but the romantic interest in castles had inspired Maximillian II of Bavaria at Hohenschwangau a generation before in 1832–6 and the Schwarzenburgs at Hluboka; as with Cardiff and Castell Coch, both these were built on medieval castle ruins.

Burgess gave Castell Coch a banqueting hall, a 'drawing room' in one of the towers, and two ornate bedrooms. The lavish decoration of these rooms and much of the furniture which Burgess designed for them remain, but the castle sadly lacks curtains or carpets or any feeling of being occupied.

Old Beaupre Castle   This ruined Elizabethan manor, adapted from a medieval house, lies in an idyllic situation on a low bluff above the small River Thaw, ten minutes' brisk walk across fields from the bridge by Howemill Farm. The workings of the estate and home farm cannot be understood at once since a farm still occupies one wing of the house and the old outbuildings. The approach is by a footpath along an old side road and not along the main formal approach road. In the fields around earthworks mark the garden and orchards.

St Lythans Burial Chamber   The fine remains of a Neolithic chambered tomb can be seen here.

Tinkinswood Burial Chamber   A badly ruined long barrow on top of a low hill with some remaining atmosphere, surrounded by wire, pylon lines, television masts, telephone cables and fences. The site was excavated in 1914 and lies in the centre of a large enclosure, overgrown with high grass and nettles. The site could be re-excavated to form a textbook example of a chambered tomb of Neolithic date.

West Glamorgan

Loughor Castle   On a mound above a Roman fort stands a single tower of this castle.

Margam Stones Museum   On the site of a Celtic monastery at the west end of the plain of Glamorgan, where the mountains almost reach the sea, stands a fine Cistercian abbey. Founded by Robert, Earl of Gloucester, Henry I's bastard, the abbey is reasonably complete and should soon be open to visitors. The nave, with remarkable family tombs and Regency embellishments, serves as the parish church while the ruins of the east end and cloister-buildings are in the grounds of Margam Park, recently purchased by the County Council and local UDC. This should be a superb place to visit, despite the savage industrial pollution and the droning traffic of the main road.

In the old school house, by the church, is a fine collection of inscribed and sculptured stones from Margam and nearby, including twelve early crosses of the fifth to twelfth centuries AD.

Neath Abbey   A fair amount remains of the Cistercian abbey founded by the Normans and sacked by the Welsh in AD 1224. Most of the remains are later in the thirteenth century. Like Furness (page 50) and Byland (page 161), Neath began as a Savignac house. The west range is most complete.

Margam Abbey
Museum, West
Glamorgan

Parc Le Breos burial
chamber, West
Glamorgan

Weobley Castle, West
Glamorgan

Parc Le Breos Burial Chamber   Good remains of a Neolithic chambered tomb
can be seen.

Swansea Castle   Undergoing restoration are some high remains of the fifteenth-century castle of the Bishops of St David's.

Weobley Castle   This very complete small family castle stands on a dramatic
hill-top on the north coast of the Gower peninsula overlooking the industrial
sprawl of Llanelli. The hall stands over the kitchen and dates from the end
of the thirteenth century. The other rooms, gatehouse and chapel date from
the fourteenth century and cluster tightly round a small courtyard.

Gwent

Caerleon   The small town of Caerleon, little more than a suburb of the large
industrial town of Newport, occupies the site of a Roman legionary fortress.
The atmosphere is seriously impinged on by very recent developments on the
skyline. Chosen as the strategic base for the occupation of South Wales, as
Chester was for North Wales, Caerleon lies at one of the lowest crossing points
of the Usk, as Chepstow lies on the Wye. The fortress was established about
AD 75 and occupied by the second Augustan Legion for the whole of the Roman
period. The defences can be traced and the fortress was the standard rectangular form with rounded corners, found throughout the Roman empire. A substantial town must have grown up outside the walls, largely to the south-west,
and here the main showplace lies, the Roman amphitheatre, excavated in 1926–
8. The amphitheatre had been called 'King Arthur's Round Table' since
medieval times, but no real evidence of these legendary associations was found.
The visitor can see the Roman amphitheatre, still fairly well preserved. An
oval arena is surrounded by the banks on which were tiers of seats, divided by
eight entrance passages. Some of the inscriptions, put up by the different
units, can still be seen on the stretch they built. The sports for which amphi-
theatres were built were far more varied than the present-day equivalent of
bull-fighting, which would have seemed quite dull to the Romans. Animal
hunts of all kinds, gladiator-fights and torture were the normal pastimes, and
sometimes sea-fights. (Fig. 4.)

The amphitheatre seems to have been in decay by the fourth century AD,
long before the end of the Roman occupation. The Roman army had changed
greatly by this time, part at least of the Second Legion was transferred to Richborough in Kent (page 93) and the tactical defence of the area depended on
the new fort at Cardiff. Of the buildings within the fortress the visitor can still

192

see a group of the barrack buildings 300 yards (260 metres) from the amphitheatre, if he is not deterred by the litter and broken glass strewn upon the asphalt approach path. The barrack-blocks epitomize the standard barrack-block found throughout the Empire. Also to be seen are the western corner turret of the fortress, a large latrine building and some of the cookhouses.

Caerwent   The small Roman town of Venta Silurum, the tribal capital of the Silures, was founded about AD 75. The southern half of the walled defences can be seen. Within the walls about two-thirds of the Roman buildings have been excavated (1777; 1845; 1899–1913; 1923), but the visitor can only see portions of two town-houses and a temple, surrounded by a caravan site. In the porch of the medieval church are a pair of Roman altars, but most of the finds from the excavations are in Newport museum.

Nearby may be seen *Llanmelin Wood* camp, an Iron Age hill-fort.

Chepstow Castle   This magnificent castle lies at the southernmost crossing of the Wye. At the heart of the castle is the great palace-tower which William FitzOsbern built within a few years of 1066, and part of the stone walls of the wards on either side are his work. Chepstow is one of the very few stone castles of early Norman times. The later work of the Clares and the Marshals added an extra section at each end so that the castle contains five sections on its long ridge beside the river and overlooking the town. From the period of Edward I's Welsh wars which saw so much building work, Roger Bigod of Framlingham (page 139) put up a range of domestic buildings in the lower bailey (1278–85) and lavishly remodelled FitzOsbern's palace. The Worcesters of Raglan carried out many alterations in the sixteenth century, but much of their work was destroyed in the Civil War or under the Commonwealth when the castle was maintained as a garrison; it was only dismantled as a fortress in 1690. The views from the ramparts are unspoilt, still looking down on the pleasant private gardens of the town, and many wild flowers grow on the wall tops.

The Port Wall, Chepstow   The medieval town wall of Chepstow (probably 1272–8) is still almost complete with the town gate across High Street, rebuilt as a prison in 1524. Seven other towers can still be traced, but three at the south end have been destroyed.

Llanthony Priory   The priory of Augustinian canons developed from a band of hermits, the first of whom was a knight who came while hunting to a ruined chapel of St David in the first decade of the twelfth century. Much of the church stands and dates from the end of the twelfth and beginning of the thirteenth

194

Chepstow Castle, Gwent

Llanthony Priory, Gwent

centuries. Some of the cloister-buildings can be traced and the west range is still inhabited. The canons' infirmary is complete and serves as the parish church, and beyond it lie several of the monastic barns and service buildings still in use in a farmyard. The large new car-park rather impinges on the tranquillity of the site in the narrow vale of Ewyas.

Llantilio Crossenny   A late medieval hunting-lodge in the park below White Castle. This may be on an earlier manorial site of the Bishops of Llandaff, associated with St Tilio whose church of Llantilio Crossenny is close by.

Monmouth Castle   The castle is tightly hemmed in by the town and still used in part for military purposes, which makes it difficult to appreciate the original siting of the castle and its dependent town to command the confluence of the Wye and Monnow.

   On one side of the parade ground can be seen the remains of a great tower or hall like the early Norman Palace Hall at Chepstow, with a medieval hall of the castle alongside. On another side of the parade ground stands the dignified classical façade of the lodging built within the castle in 1673 by the second Marquis of Worcester who became first Duke of Beaufort. The interior contains very rich plasterwork and can be visited on occasion. Later Badminton became the family seat and Monmouth was largely abandoned.

Little survives of the defences of the town itself, but the Monnow Gate stands on the Monnow bridge, where it defended the outer suburbs of the town. It should not be missed by the visitor.

Newport Castle   Only the impressive fourteenth- or fifteenth-century façade survives on the muddy and tidal Usk, in the centre of the large modern industrial town, first mentioned as Novus Burgus in 1126. It is sandwiched between road and railway bridges, while the rest of the castle has been encroached on by modern road widening and deep sewers. The ruins are in poor condition with shrubs and trees growing on them.

Raglan Castle   This magnificent late medieval castle is very much a showplace, often over-run by coach parties. The early castle of the Bloets was no doubt on the present site, but the earliest remains date from the time of Sir William ap Thomas, the Blue Knight of Gwent who fought at Agincourt. His son, Sir William Herbert, first Earl of Pembroke, a great Yorkist magnate in the 1460s, built almost the whole of what we see.

During the Civil War, Raglan was a Royalist stronghold which held out for two months after the surrender of Oxford. The family, recovering their estates by the restoration, built firstly Great Castle House, Monmouth, and later Badminton. The damage of the siege was followed by the deliberate slighting of the great tower and later casual looting. The castle was a well-known Romantic antiquity already by the Regency period.

The great tower can be compared with Tattershall (*c.* 1430) and Ashby de la Zouche (*c.* 1480), but harks back to the idea of a great keep of Norman times. The wrecked oriel windows of the fountain court had a striking similarity with Thornbury, Gloucestershire, whose builder, the Duke of Buckingham, was brother-in-law to the Sir Walter Herbert who held Raglan from 1491 to 1507.

Runston Chapel   The extensive earthworks of a deserted medieval village are not easy to pick out among the bracken and shrubs. They surround a Norman village chapel which stands roofless, on a low hill with sweeping views. There are no signs and no access or public right of way; the fences are of barbed wire.

The Three Castles   *Grosmont Castle* stands on a hill-top beside the pleasant village, which is well worth a visit. It was laid out to be a town originally, but only the handsome cruciform church and the delightful miniature town hall indicate its former urban status. The castle itself was rather a garrisoned strong-

Raglan Castle, Gwent

point than a residential castle and consists of a single ward with typical early thirteenth-century circular drum-towers, one side of which is formed by a hybrid block, something between a keep and a hall. The site is well defended by a deep moat and the present wire fence.

Skenfrith Castle is the second of the three castles which, together with Grosmont and White Castle, commanded the rich arable land of the middle Monnow valley. Skenfrith Castle seems to have been built during the short-lived lordship of Hubert de Burgh who held the district in 1201–5 and 1219–32. It is on the site of an earlier Norman earthwork castle. The castle is nearly rectangular with a round tower at each corner, resembling a typical garrison fort of many periods and regions. In the middle stands a large round tower or keep, no doubt

198

copied from Pembroke, and is typical of South Wales. The village lies pleasantly among wooded hills and has a fine large church of the same period as the castle.

White Castle, the last of the three, had a more complicated history. After 1254 it was in royal hands. The castle dominates a wide area and has fine panoramic views from its hill-top.

There is no trace of an early Norman motte-and-bailey castle. From late Norman times there survive the foundations of a small stone keep such as that at Goodrich and the high curtain wall of the inner ward. In *c.* 1260 the keep was demolished and drum towers and a great gateway added to the curtain wall, and at the same time a large outer ward was fortified. All this work has a clearly military character as a frontier fortress at that period. The very deep water-filled moats and the 'hornwork' are remarkable.

Tintern Abbey This Cistercian abbey was founded in AD 1113 by Walter de Clare, Lord of Chepstow, in a remote site among the rocky cliffs of the Wye, a typical Cistercian outlook. The original buildings were rebuilt on quite a grand scale between 1270 and 1301 by Roger Bigod, Earl of Norfolk, whose domestic ranges survive at Chepstow (page 194), and the monastic buildings were extensively reconstructed in late medieval times. Tintern was never among the richest of monastic houses but enjoyed a peaceful prosperity.

The abbey has been popular with visitors since the eighteenth century, and the wild and beautiful scenery has always appealed to the romantic. Almost every detail of a large monastic establishment can be picked out in foundations beside the dominating remains of the church. It is a great pity, however, that large car-parks have had to be laid out in the centre of the monastic precinct and that a row of superb 'new residences' has been allowed to overlook the abbey.

Gwynedd

Early Prehistoric Sites, Anglesey The island of Anglesey has a great number of monuments in state hands. They are mostly small, scattered and not easy to relate to a pattern of settlement or to a sequence of cultural development; many are attractively sited and well worth visiting.

The most numerous are the earliest. From the long period of the first settled cultivators in about the fourth to the second millennium BC there are eight burial sites, a sacred enclosure, two isolated standing stones and a pair of standing stones. The burial sites are best understood from *Barclodiad y Gawres* (not always open), magnificently sited on the west coast of the island, and *Bryn Celli Ddu*, not far from the Menai bridge. The former has a cross-plan stone chamber in the centre of a round mound, very much like Irish chamber tombs.

Some of the stones have zig-zag and spiral decorations pecked on. The latter, which seems to be built over a sacred enclosure, has a stone chamber and entrance passage and one stone decorated with wavy lines. The other sites have been less thoroughly studied: the burial chambers are left, but the mounds have gone. Pairs of chambers survive at *Din Dryfol* and *Presaddfed*, both fairly close to *Barclodiad y Gawres*. Also close is *Ty Newydd* where only one of a pair of chambers survives. Another complex example is *Trefignath* on Holyhead, with a long divided passage. *Bodowyr* near the Menai Strait and *Lligwy* on the east coast have very imposing single chambers. The sacred enclosure, *Castell Bryn Gwyn*, near the Menai Strait was later altered to form a defended homestead. The standing stones may be surviving fragments of stone circles or cairns. They are all in the north-west of Anglesey. On Holyhead the pair at *Penrhos Feilw* and one at *Ty Mawr* are all at least 10 feet (3 metres) high, while the one at *Tregwehelydd* is slightly shorter.

Bodowyr burial
chamber, Anglesey

A hill-fort, perhaps of late prehistoric date, *Caer y Twr* is on the summit of Holyhead Mountain. Homesteads occupied mostly in the Roman period form a large group on the south-west flank of *Holyhead Mountain*. There is a single small homestead-enclosure at *Caer Leb* near the Menai Strait and a larger one at *Din Lligwy* on the east coast. Foundations of both road and rectangular huts can be seen at all three sites.

Caer Gybi, a small late Roman fort within which stands the parish church at Holyhead, is partly in state care.

On the eastern tip of Anglesey at *Penmon* is a group of later monuments. A fine carved *cross* of about the tenth century AD, rather lost in the middle of a potato field, stands above an early Christian site, where the sacred *well* of St Seiriol has a well-house, perhaps partly of fourteenth-, partly of seventeenth-century date. Cut into the limestone cliff close by is the supposed 'cell' of the saint, which looks very like a Georgian lime-kiln. Beside the parish church is the roofless shell of the cloister-building of a small Augustinian *priory*, which developed out of a Celtic monastery on Priestholm, a small island just out to sea. Across the road is a fine Jacobean *dovecot* built for a nearby estate.

North of Penmon on the east coast of Anglesey, near one of the burial chambers and a Roman farmstead, is *Capel Lligwy*, the shell of a twelfth-century chapel with later alterations.

Beaumaris Castle, Anglesey　With this mass of small sites, Anglesey has one surprise: at Beaumaris is one of the largest and finest of European castles. It is far from complete since only the lower half of the main walls and towers was ever built, just enough to be defensible. The castle lies just outside the small holiday-town, not at all as dominating as Conwy (page 205) or Caernarfon (page 202). Beaumaris lacks the rocky crag of Harlech (page 209) and barely dominates the flat coastal plain and the Strait. It was the last of Edward I's great North Wales castles, begun after the desperate Welsh revolt of 1294 when Caernarfon was taken. What we see was almost all built in 1295–6 by Edward's engineers from Savoy; they brought an English workforce of 2,500 men, while the King himself was off on his first Scottish conquest and his disastrous expedition to the Low Countries. This final spendthrift castle-building gave the engineers the chance to try another variation of the symmetrical plan of Rhuddlan (page 180). Beaumaris has opposed gatehouses on two sides and six great towers in the main wall. The low outer wall, which was finished, has two lesser gatehouses, twelve small towers and a fortified dock.

Caernarfon Castle　The grandest and the cruellest of Edward I's castles was started in 1283, captured and sacked in a Welsh revolt in 1294 and continued in 1295–9 and 1304–27: forty-four years' work at a cost of about £20,000, with

another £7,000 spent on the walls, gates, quays, bridges and mill-ponds for the town of English colonists beside the castle.

Caernarfon, the 'Fort in Arfon', was the ancient capital of Gwynedd and a previous conquest in early Norman times had resulted in a motte-and-bailey castle here. There may have been a trading-port where the town is now, with the princes' seat of government in the Roman fort 700 yards (600 metres) inland (see page 204) and the church-centre of the district about 230 yards (200 metres) beyond at St Peblig's church.

Quite unlike the other North Wales castles, which have round towers and plain walling, Caernarfon Castle has angled towers and banded walling, a deliberate echo of the Theodosian wall of Constantinople, whose founder Constantine was associated in ancient Welsh legend with Caernarfon. In this way Edward I and his advisers were trying to mark out Caernarfon as a 'new Rome': it stands for their ambition of imperial power.

The castle coldly expresses ruthless power in its gigantic scale and perfection of design and proportion—the work of a government committee at its very best. But the men who accomplished this grim masterpiece were not English. The first constable was the King's closest friend, Sir Otto de Grandson; the whole design was made by Master James of St George. They and many others in Edward's entourage were advisers and adventurers from Savoy (now split up between France, Italy and Switzerland), where the King's nephew was Count. Though it was designed as a palace-castle, few of the buildings within were ever built, and they have all gone. The interior formed a marvellous scene for the pageantry of the Investiture of the Prince of Wales. Towers, arrow-slits and passages seem endless.

Caernarfon (Segontium) Roman Fort The northern half of a permanent Roman military garrison is on show rather dismally: the foundations of the 'Roman' buildings are mostly modern replicas, the fort-wall is represented by a shabby fence, its ditches by a belt of overgrown land. An imaginative redesign could do wonders.

The fort was surrounded in Roman times by a large civil settlement and the nearby church of St Peblig probably stands in a Roman cemetery and may have developed from a late Roman mausoleum or shrine. Medieval legend suggests that the site was important in early Christian times.

Capel Garmon, Llanrwst A long barrow with three chambers.

Castell y Bere On a rocky knoll in a remote side valley of the Dysinni lies this small castle, apparently of *c.* 1221–94. There is no evidence earlier than Llewelyn the Great, and no signs of what happened to Edward I's garrison

in the Welsh rising of 1294 beyond abundant burning found when the site was dug.

Conwy Castle   One of the most perfect of medieval castles, with its town walls attached, Conwy lies on the west bank of the broad sheltered estuary of the River Conwy facing the low peaks of Deganwy, an ancient Welsh stronghold which had been rebuilt in the mid thirteenth century as an English frontier castle. Edward I and his team of advisers from Savoy planned Conwy in 1283 to be the largest English town on the North Wales coast, protected by its castle, perched on a rocky hill at the water's edge. Pushed ahead at great speed and vast expense, the main works were finished within five years, a complete contrast to Caernarfon which was begun a few months later and left unfinished until almost fifty years later.

Conwy's strategic value as a link was very great, but the farmlands of the

Castell y Bere,
Gwynedd

20 North Wales: (*top*) the Roman conquest involved large garrisons in forts sited usuall
at the heads of the cultivated valleys, linked by a network of roads which is not completel
known; (*bottom*) the English conquest was based on very massive castles with small garri
sons, which commanded the valleys from the coast and could be supplied by sea

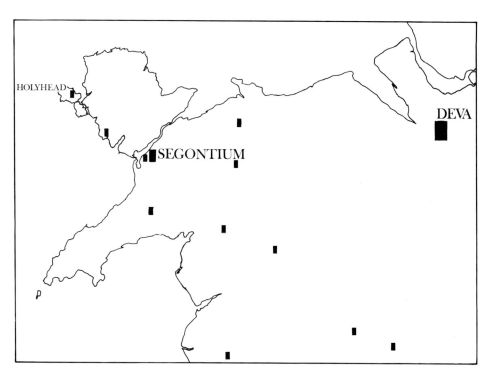

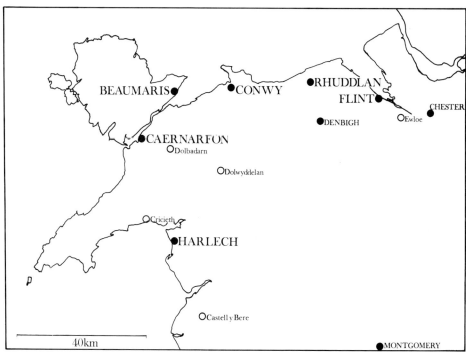

narrow Conwy valley can never have supported as large a population as the low cornlands of Anglesey or the broad coastal plain round Caernarfon, where most of the resources of Gwynedd were focused. This 'instant' fortress was built by a very large team of craftsmen drafted in from every English county, some under armed guard to deter deserters. Many of the detailed works-files of the office-teams survive in the Public Records, and bear witness to a very efficient bureaucracy.

The castle, with its distinctive eight-towered silhouette, occupies a cramped site and is not as large as many other major castles. The main interior buildings are intact except for floors and roofs, and the broad rampart-walk gives a very good panorama of the inside workings and outside setting of the castle. The most difficult change to grasp is that below the steep modern access-ramp and its fine rock garden there used to be a broad moat between the castle and the town.

The circuit of the town walls is very complete and reminiscent of some South German town defences, which is hardly surprising since the designer of Conwy was Master James of St George, from Savoy on the borders of Switzerland and France. The visitor should not miss several fine houses and the church, which began as a Cistercian abbey older than the town. This whole great work bankrupted half the banking-system of Europe, and in 1293 Edward I defaulted on his loans from Italian bankers. (Fig. 4.)

Cricieth Castle The most stunning and exhilarating of all the wonderfully poetic castles of the Welsh princes, Cricieth stands on a sudden vast rocky promontory, and we can almost forget the squalor of caravans and the dreadful concrete ramp up. This may have been a prehistoric fortress and was later the main stronghold of Eifionydd.

The castle fell in the main English conquest of 1283. It was soon reconstructed and the impressive gatehouse built, while the town of English colonists was established in 1284. Cricieth was held against the rebels in 1294 when we have the commander's receipts for goods shipped in. In 1404 the rebel Owain Glyndwr took the castle, burnt it out, and it was never repaired.

Cymmer Abbey Of the small Cistercian abbey, something of the church and the cloisters can be picked out, but this monument is badly imposed upon.

Dinorwic Slate Quarry A museum has been opened up within the chaos of one of the last slate quarries to show its foundries, smithies, workshops and railways.

Dolbadarn Castle Dramatically sited between the lakes are the low walls of one of the princes' strongholds. In the centre a great round tower reminds us of Pembroke.

Dolwyddelan Castle   On a high knoll among impressive wooded country are the keep and some of the walls of another small castle of the princes.

Dyffryn Long Barrow   A badly ruined long barrow with two chambers can be seen behind the school.

Fedw-Deg   A late medieval hall.

Gwydir Uchaf Chapel   A chapel of 1673, for the mansion.

Harlech Castle   This famous and imposing castle was built in a few years (1283–90) and planned to command the west side of Snowdonia when Edward I decided to do away with the unruly princes of North Wales. Harlech has a towered main gatehouse and four round corner-towers in the main circuit of wall above a low outer wall, standing on a great rock high above the flat marshland. This was all sea when the castle was built and it could be provisioned by ship.
   Harlech withstood the rebellious Welsh who captured Caernarfon in 1294,

but was starved out by the rebel Owain Glyndwr, who held it in 1404–9. In later troubles Harlech was the last Lancastrian garrison to hold out in 1468 and the last Cavalier garrison in 1647.

The grim and imposing stronghold still looms on its rock.

Llangar   A small late medieval church.

Llangybi   A well-chamber attributed to St Cybi.

Penarth Fawr   A hall house of *c*. 1400.

Powys

Brecon Gaer   A Roman fort of the early second century AD stands on a low rise in the fertile valley of the upper Usk with a fine rural situation behind a farmyard and below the A40. The south and west walls are nicely overgrown and thickety; the west and south gates and north-east corner tower are carefully exposed inside small fenced enclosures.

Although the fort was abandoned in *c*. AD 140, a civil settlement on flat land towards the north and east may have remained. In early Christian times the fort was traditionally the birthplace of St Brychan who may have founded the church which is now Brecon Cathedral, 2 miles (3 km.) to the east. The nearby hill-forts of Pen-y-crug and Slwch Tumb were clearly regional centres at various times. The latter is the burial place of St Brychan's daughter, St Alud. The site is marvellously unsignposted.

Bronllys Castle   On the shoulder of a hill dominating the confluence of three tributaries, 2 miles (3 km.) south of the Wye, stand the remains of a small garrison castle of the Cliffords. Only the thirteenth-century tower standing on a Norman motte can be visited. The bailey on the flatter land behind has been levelled for the lawn of the pleasant Georgian house.

Bryntail Lead Mine   A monument of nineteenth-century industrial archaeology preserving buildings and settling tanks.

Dolforwyn Castle   A completely ruined Welsh castle built by Llywelyn ap Gruffydd in 1273.

Montgomery Castle   Montgomery Castle was built by Henry III in 1223–7. Excavations have revealed two main wards of the castle. The old castle, Hen Domen, is a fine motte-and-bailey earthwork $\frac{1}{2}$ mile (1 km.) to the north nearer

the Severn ford. Very important excavations here have revealed many details of Roger of Montgomery's first stronghold. He was one of William the Conqueror's closest circle and refounded Wenlock Priory (page 129).

Tretower Castle and Court   Extensive remains of both the early medieval castle and the late medieval manor-house which succeeded it, a couple of hundred yards away, can be visited. Tretower succeeds the Roman fort of Pen y Gaer and the older Welsh settlement of Llanfihangel Cwmdu as the centre of the Rhian-goll valley, a side stream of the middle Usk. The early Norman castle of Picard consisted of a motte-and-bailey, but the bailey is largely covered by new farm buildings and cannot be visited. The motte was used as the base for a powerful shell keep in *c.* 1150. This had a circle of rooms, the outer walls of which survive in part to a great height. But the middle was demolished in *c*. 1230 and replaced by a great circular tower on the pattern of Pembroke Castle.

The nearby Tretower Court is entered through a gatehouse set in a battlemented wall which gives an appearance of a miniature castle, but this was built entirely for show as a glance at the back of the house, which is entirely domestic in character, will show. (Fig. 6.)

On the right of the courtyard is the fourteenth-century hall-range which was reconstructed in the fifteenth century and converted into chambers with a galleried front.

It should be noted that many of the visible features in both stone and wood are modern restorations on the lines of ancient work of several periods. This is quite at variance with the Department's usual practice of conservative restoration.

Index

Index

Abbotsbury Abbey, 61
Abingdon County Hall, 124
Acton Burnell Castle, 128
Aldborough Roman town, 161
Anglesey, prehistoric and Roman, 199
Anglo-Saxon kings and nobles, 75, 104, 129, 139
Appledore chapel, 85
Appuldurcombe House, 82
Arthur's Stone, Dorstone, 160
Ashby de la Zouche Castle, 96
Audley End House, 70
Avebury, early sites, 148
Aylesford barrows, 85

Baconsthorpe Castle, 30, 107
Barnard Castle, 67
Basingwerk Abbey, 179
Bayham Abbey, 141
Beaumaris Castle, 201
Beeston Castle, 39
Belas Knap barrow, 74
Berkhamsted Castle, 84
Berney Arms Windmill, 107
Berwick on Tweed ramparts, 28, 113
Binham Priory, 108
Bishop Auckland deer-house, 68
Bishop's Waltham Palace, 77
Blackbury hill-fort, 57
Blakeney Guildhall, 108
Bolingbroke Castle, 98
Bolsover Castle, 55
Boscobel House, 128
Bowes Castle, 68
Bradford on Avon barn, 155
Bratton hill-fort and horse, 156
Brecon Roman fort, 210
Brinkburn Priory, 113
Bristol, church, 37
Bronllys Castle, 210
Brough Castle, 50
Brougham Castle, 50

Bryntail lead mine, 210
Buildwas Abbey, 128
Burgh Castle Roman fort, 137
Burton Agnes Hall, 85
Bury St Edmund's Abbey, 24, 139
Byland Abbey, 161

Caerleon Roman fort, 28, 192
Caernarfon: Roman fort, castle and town walls, 202
Caerphilly Castle, 185
Caerwent Roman town, 194
Caister by Yarmouth Roman town, 108
Callington well-chapel, 44
Canterbury, abbey and church, 86
Capel Garmon barrow, 204
Carew cross, 181
Carisbrooke Roman fort and Castle, 82
Carreg Cennen Castle, 181
Castell Coch, castle, 187
Castell y Bere, castle, 204
Castle Acre Priory and gate, 24, 108
Castlerigg stone circle, 50
Castle Rising, castle, 109
Castleton, castle, 56
Chale lighthouse-chapel, 83
Charlcombe monument, 37
Charles II and his times, 61, 70, 73, 81, 95, 98, 99, 104, 128, 196
Chepstow Castle and town walls, 194
Chester Roman amphitheatre and Castle, 41
Chirk, gates, 179
Christchurch Castle, 63
Cilgerran Castle, 87, 181
Civil War, 37, 38, 41, 47, 56, 59, 65, 67, 96, 107, 132, 141, 158, 171, 194, 197, 210
Cleeve Abbey, 130
Coity Castle, 186
Colchester, prehistoric and monastic, 70

Conisbrough Castle, 173
Conwy Castle and town walls, 28, 205
Cornwall, prehistoric and Roman, 44
Creake Abbey, 109
Cricieth Castle, 208
Croxden Abbey, 136
Cumbria, prehistoric sites, 53
Cymmer Abbey, 208

Dartmouth Castle and battery, 57
Deal Castle, 29, 87
Deddington Castle, 124
Deerhurst chapel, 74
Denbigh Castle, town walls and
    churches, 179
Denny Abbey, 39
Derbyshire, prehistoric, 55
Derwen cross, 179
Dinorwic slate-quarry, 208
Dolbadarn Castle, 208
Dolforwyn Castle, 210
Dolwyddelan Castle, 209
Dorset, prehistoric sites, 63
Dover Castle and church, 87
Dunstanburgh Castle, 113
Dunster market, cross and bridge, 130
Duxford chapel, 39
Dyffryn barrow, 209
Dymchurch Martello tower, 90

Easby Abbey, 27, 164
Ebbsfleet monument, 90
Edward I and his times, 48, 84, 88, 103,
    104, 111, 128, 139, 179, 180, 181,
    185, 194, 199, 202, 204, 205, 208,
    209
Edward II, 113
Edward III and his times, 72, 104, 181
Egglestone Abbey, 69
Elizabeth I and her times, 28, 47, 48,
    50, 67, 73, 76, 83, 95, 101, 111, 113,
    128, 139, 145, 158, 179, 189
Ewenny Priory, 186
Ewloe Castle, 179
Eynsford Castle, 30, 90

Farleigh Hungerford Castle, 130
Farnham Castle, 141

Fedw-Deg house, 209
Finchale Priory, 69
Flint Castle, 179
Fountains Abbey, 164
Fowey, battery, 44
Framlingham Castle, 139
Furness Abbey, 50

Geddington cross, 111
Gisborough Priory, 44
Glastonbury tribunal and barn, 132
Glamorgan, barrows, 189
Gloucestershire, prehistoric sites, 74,
    77
Goodrich Castle, 160
Great Yarmouth, friary and houses, 109
Grime's Graves flint-mine, 110
Grosmont Castle, 197
Gwydir Uchaf chapel, 209

Hadleigh Castle, 37
Hailes Abbey, 77
Hardknot Roman fort, 52
Hardwick Old Hall, 56
Harlech Castle, 209
Haughmond Abbey, 128
Helmsley Castle, 166
Henry I and his times, 39, 65, 66, 77,
    80, 145, 157, 179, 189, 199
Henry II and his times, 31, 39, 50, 56,
    68, 72, 73, 74, 84, 88, 90, 95, 111,
    130, 139, 141, 161, 164, 166, 168,
    169, 171
Henry III and his times, 39, 46, 48, 72,
    77, 80, 82, 84, 89, 103, 109, 143,
    145, 161, 181, 194, 198, 210
Henry VIII and his times, 29, 44, 46,
    59, 79, 80, 81, 82, 83, 87, 100, 101,
    104, 116, 141, 145
Herringfleet Priory, 139
Higham Ferrers college, 111
Holywell chapel, 179
Houghton House, 37
Hound Tor hamlet, 59
Howden church, 85
Hurst Castle, 79
Hurstmonceaux Castle, 142
Hylton Castle, 143

Isleham Priory, 39

Jarrow Priory, 143
John and his times, 89, 90, 93, 171
Jordan Hill Roman temple, 63

Kenilworth Castle, 145
Kent, prehistoric sites, 85
Kidwelly Castle, 181
King Doniert's Stone, St Cleer, 44
Kings Wood Abbey gatehouse, 77
Kirby Hall, 111
Kirby Muxloe Castle, 29, 97
Kirkham Priory, 166
Knowlton Circle and church, 63

Lamphey, Bishop's Palace, 182
Lanercost Priory, 53
Launceston Castle, 44
Leicester Roman forum, 97
Leiston Abbey, 139
Lilleshall Abbey, 24, 128
Lincoln, Bishop's Palace, 98
Lindisfarne Priory, 115
Lindsey chapel, 141
Llangar church, 210
Llangybi holy well, 210
Llanstephan Castle, 183
Llanthony Priory, 194
Llantilio Crossenny moat, 196
Llawhaden Castle, 183
London, palaces and royal sites, 98–105
Longthorpe Tower, 30, 39
Loughor Castle, 189
Lullingstone Roman villa, 90
Lyddington Bedehouse, 97
Lydford Castle, 59

Maiden Castle hill-fort, 28, 63
Margam Stones Museum, 189
Mattersey Priory, 124
Meare fish-house, 132
Middleham Castle, 29, 166
Minster Lovell Hall, 125
Mistley church towers, 73
Monk Bretton Priory, 173
Monmouth Castle, 196
Montgomery Castle, 210

Moreton Corbet Castle, 128
Mortimer's Cross watermill, 161
Mount Grace Priory, 168
Muchelney Abbey, 133

Neath Abbey, 189
Netheravon dovecot, 156
Netley Priory, 27, 80
Newcastle Bridgend, 185
Newport Castle, 197
Norham Castle, 116
North Elmham Cathedral, 110
North Leigh Roman villa, 125
Norwich tower, 111
Nunney Castle, 30, 136

Ogmore Castle, 187
Okehampton Castle, 60
Old Beaupre Manor, 189
Old Oswestry hill-fort, 128
Old Sarum hill-fort and town, 157
Old Soar Manor, 91
Old Wardour Castle, 157
Orford Castle, 141
Osborne House, 83
Ospringe hospital, 91

Paignton priest's house, 61
Penarth Fawr house, 210
Pendennis Castle, 46
Penrith Castle, 53
Pentre Ifan barrow, 183
Pevensey Roman fort and Castle, 142
Plymouth Citadel, 61
Portchester Roman fort and Castle, 80
Portsmouth hospital and gates, 80

Raglan Castle, 197
Reculver Roman fort and church towers, 91
Restormel Castle, 48
Rhuddlan Castles, 180
Richard I, 80
Richborough Roman fort, 93
Richmond Castle, 169
Rievaulx Abbey, 24, 169
Roche Abbey, 24, 173
Rochester Castle, 93

217

Roger, Bishop of Salisbury, 39, 65, 66, 77, 157
Rotherwas chapel, 161
Rufford Abbey, 124
Runston chapel, 197
Rushton Lodge, 111
Rycote chapel, 125

St Albans Roman walls, 84
St David's walls and chapel, 183
St Dogmael's Abbey, 183
St Mawes Castle, 46
Salley Abbey, 96
Sandbach crosses, 41
Saxtead Mill, 141
Scarborough Castle, 169
Scilly Isles, 48
Segontium Roman fort, 204
Shap Abbey, 53
Sherborne Castle, 65
Shropshire, prehistoric sites, 128
Skenfrith Castle, 197
Skipsea Castle, 85
Spofforth Castle, 172
Stanton Drew stone circles, 136
Stanwick prehistoric fortress, 172
Steeton Hall gatehouse, 172
Stephen, 50, 77, 173
Stonehenge, 152
Stoney Littleton barrow, 37
Strata Florida Abbey, 185
Strood Manor, 95
Swansea Castle, 192

Talley Abbey, 185
Thetford Priory and Lodge, 111
Thornton Abbey, 85
Tilbury Fort, 73
Tintagel Castle, 48
Tintern Abbey, 199

Titchfield Abbey, 82
Totnes Castle, 29, 61
Tretower Castle and house, 30, 211
Tynemouth Priory and defences, 143

Uffington hill-fort, 127
Upnor Castle, 95

Valle Crucis Abbey and cross, 180

Wall Roman baths, 137
Walmer Castle, 87
Waltham Abbey remains, 73
Warkworth Castle, 116
Warton house, 96
Waverley Abbey, 141
Wayland's Smithy barrow, 127
Weeting house, 111
Wenlock Priory, 27, 129
Weobley Castle, 192
West Malling Castle, 96
Whalley Abbey gatehouse, 96
Wheeldale Moor Roman road, 172
Whitby Abbey, 27, 172
White Ladies Priory, 128
Whitford cross, 181
William I and his times, 31, 44, 46, 56, 67, 75, 84, 87, 88, 103, 108, 109, 111, 129, 139, 142, 160, 169, 180, 194, 211
William II, 50, 104, 143
Wiltshire, prehistoric sites, 145
Windsor Castle, 39
Witcombe Roman villa, 77
Wrest Park garden and pavilions, Silsoe, 37
Wroxeter Roman town, 129

Yarmouth Castle, 83
York castle-keep, 173

218